THE MARCH TO CAPITALISM IN THE TRANSITION COUNTRIES

Other books by Irving S. Michelman:

Consumer Finance: A Case History in American Business
Business at Bay: Critics and Heretics of American Business
The Crisis Meeters: Business Response to Social Crises
The Roots of Capitalism in Western Civilization: A Socioeconomic
    Assessment
The Moral Limitations of Capitalism

The March to Capitalism in the Transition Countries

IRVING S. MICHELMAN
Former corporate executive and advisor to Federal Reserve Board and US Department of Commerce

Routledge
Taylor & Francis Group

LONDON AND NEW YORK

First published 1998 by Ashgate Publishing

Reissued 2018 by Routledge
2 Park Square, Milton Park, Abingdon, Oxon, OX14 4RN
52 Vanderbilt Avenue, New York, NY 10017

Routledge is an imprint of the Taylor & Francis Group, an informa business

Publisher's Note
The publisher has gone to great lengths to ensure the quality of this reprint but points out that some imperfections in the original copies may be apparent.

Disclaimer
The publisher has made every effort to trace copyright holders and welcomes correspondence from those they have been unable to contact.

A Library of Congress record exists under LC control number: 98071401

Typeset in Breeze Limited, Manchester

ISBN 13: 978-1-138-33647-6 (hbk)
ISBN 13: 978-1-138-33648-3 (pbk)
ISBN 13: 978-0-429-44299-5 (ebk)

For Shirley

Contents

Acknowledgements

My thanks to Robert Heilbroner, a generous advisor whose clarity of expression and independence of intellect have expanded the history and practise of economic thought. Others who were gracious and helpful are James D. Wolfensohn, president of the World Bank, Daniel Citrin, head of the Russian Division of the International Monetary Fund, Marshall Goldman of Harvard's Center for Russian Studies, and Larry Summers, US Deputy Secretary of the Treasury. I also express thanks to Anna Freimanova, assistant to President Václav Havel of the Czech Republic, and to my wife for her patience and critical eye.

Introduction

The aim of this book is to analyze and reconsider one of the great economic dramas of Western history, the march to capitalism in Russia, the once-feared superpower, and in three important, long-occupied, former Soviet satellites, Hungary, Poland, and the Czech Republic. The period is from 1989 on, after the fall of the Berlin Wall, when the liberated countries rushed headlong into democracy and capitalism. The word capitalism is used frequently herein rather than market-system. There was a deeply-felt need in the above countries to reject economic socialism as the accomplice of political totalitarianism. Capitalism signifies a complete change from socialism in its private ownership of property and enterprise. The market-system, while an important technique of capitalism, focuses on keeping the state at arm's length from business and industry.

A special emphasis of this book is on the role, often little-understood, played by the Western-dominated international-aid agencies, the International Monetary Fund and the World Bank, both poorly-named, but essential to the transition. They were called in while the Western countries dawdled and made empty promises. They basically financed and guided the transition, their own funds amounting to $50 billion, while issuing market-system strictures in the process. This attitude reflected the supremacy of such ideology, which reached a high-tide of approval, based on its unquestioned performance, in the Thatcher-Reagan era. Russia, in its agony, offers a laboratory for the conflicting claims of free-market theory against a more pragmatic, experimental approach.

* * *

xi

Another force reverberates throughout this book. China, whose transition now occupies the world's attention, because of its prodigious economic growth, holds implications for all competitors in the future. China's change dates from Deng Xiaoping's takeover in 1978. In his unabashed borrowing from capitalism and the market-system, while staying loyal to authoritarian rule, Deng left China a puzzle as well as a paragon. We can now reconsider Russia's shock treatment in the light of China's pragmatic gradualism.

Additionally this book is concerned with great historic figures, such as Gorbachev and Yeltsin, and Mao and Deng. It examines the personalities and programs of academic economists coming into their own in terms of power, notably Harvard's Jeffrey Sachs, Russia's Yegor Gaidar, and Poland's Leszek Balcerowicz. It also deals with a philosopher-president, Václav Havel, toughened by prison, ruminating about a more human face for the capitalism he has conditionally approved, and with Adam Michnik, Poland's dissident editor, an early participant in the Solidarity movement.

Special attention is paid to Russia's large corporations, reflecting the author's background as a corporate executive and government advisor, and author of previous books on various aspects of capitalism. Accordingly, Gazprom, Russia's largest employer, with a 375,000 workforce, 60% privatized from the socialist days, reappears throughout the book as a prototype for Russia's mixed economic results.

* * *

Finally, in considering the changing role of the state in the global-economy, we maintain that capitalism, like democracy, should be valued for its pluralism. It is not a theology. It rightfully offers a hard-won, pragmatic spectrum of choice, based on a country's needs, traditions, and stage of growth.

1 Russia: Lurching Towards Capitalism

The Aim of This Book

This book analyzes and reconsiders the march to capitalism in Russia and in three important former Soviet-occupied countries, Hungary, Poland, and the Czech Republic, during the recent post-Cold War period. It also examines the march in China, certainly a transition country, but unlikely to end in capitalism, as in the four European countries.

The literature on the transition economies, particularly that of Russia and the three Eastern restored democracies, is ample, responding to fast-moving developments.[1] A close analogy to Russia's transition literature would be that of the New Deal. The New Deal was similarly propelled by a cataclysmic event, replete with pain, suffering, and loss of status, strategized by youthful brain-trusters, marked by grand experiments and failures, great personalities and harsh demagoguery, and finally terminated by a process of muddling through. A residual question from the agony of America's Depression is who saved capitalism? For Russia, the transition question may well be what kind of capitalism was saved?

* * *

Make no mistake about it: Russia has succeeded in lurching from socialism to capitalism. There is little if any chance it will revert to its seventy-year trajectory as the fear-inspiring, totally-centralized economy that worked well enough to challenge the Western profit

1

system. Khrushchev's threat to bury capitalism has vanished. Russia, the struggling survivor of the collapsed Soviet empire, has formally and substantively joined the opposition.

Reflections of a Distressed President

As 1996 ended, President Yeltsin, recovering from serious illness, could wonder when Russia would emerge from its chronic economic problems. He had barely won his re-election, but was still losing the economic war. Inflation continued, gross domestic product was less than that of 1991, his takeover year, crime and corruption were rampant, and his tax-collection system was in a shambles. The fruits of capitalism were bitter, with pensions unpaid, the state unable to meet its budgets, and the International Monetary Fund actually suspending Russia's $340 million monthly payments, on funds already authorized, the penalty for non-compliance.

On the other hand, the distressed president could contemplate three remarkable signs on the economic horizon. First, from the calculating world of money and risk, a group of world-class investment bankers underwrote and easily sold $1 billion of Russian government bonds in the Eurobond market on November 23, the first public debt issue of a Russian government since the czars raised hundreds of millions on bond certificates destined to end as wallpaper.[2] The Eurobond rate was a respectable 9¼%, with five-year maturity, compared with the 40% or more short-term rates being charged by Russia's unruly commercial bankers, most of whom prefer to make high-rate loans to shady speculators, invest in embarrassingly high-yield government treasury bills, or buy into auctions and foreclosures of shares in privatized large corporations, rather than finance the thousands of creditworthy entre-preneurs unleashed by privatization. Five hundred of these rogue banks are reportedly marked for extinction by the harassed govern-ment, slow to learn the minimum rules of regulated capitalism, while still in awe of unfettered market capitalism.

Gazprom: A Transition Paradigm

The second economic triumph to savor was the initial public offering to foreign investors, in October 1996, of shares in Gazprom, Russia's natural resources treasure and the world's largest natural gas provider. Only a fractional 1.15% of Gazprom's shares were offered. They netted $415 million and were oversubscribed fivefold. Foreign funds, whether from Eurobond sales or from selling to foreigners shares of state-owned property, are a high priority for cash-starved Russia, unable to pay on time its threadbare army, including 1,000 generals still hanging in. Above all, the funds are non-inflationary, going to the central bank, or in Gazprom's case, the corporate entity, which owed at time of sale $2.8 billion in back taxes to the government, in turn desperately committed to reducing six straight years of very high, inflationary budget deficits.[3]

In addition, foreign investment, like foreign aid and favorable trade balances, offsets what the macrostabilization economists, who specialize in the total picture of national outflows and inflows, call capital flight. Capital flight in this case is nothing but the remittances of Russian wealth, preferably in dollars, sent by hasty and ingenious connivers to Swiss banks and other havens, under the quickly-learned market maxim of money first. The flight from 1992 to 1994 was well over $50 billion, from a high of $25 billion at the outset to about $10 billion in 1994. A top strategy of transition reformers in Russia at the start of 1992 was to declare the battered ruble freely convertible, a tough-minded tactic claimed necessary for engaging in the market world of open trade and finance, come what may. In a sense, it was a reversal of Roosevelt's emergency post-inaugural bank-closing, the ban on further flight of gold bullion, and the end of time-honored currency convertibility into gold by citizens. But then America was on the gold standard, the banking system was at stake, and the country was paralyzed with fear. Passionate free-market ideology was also in disrepute.

* * *

Back to Gazprom, a classic paradigm for illustrating the complex issues surrounding Russia's uneasy transition to capitalism. Historically it recalls the great natural resources, oil, gas, nickel, sometimes diamonds and gold, that sustained the old Soviet economic system. Selling such assets through the state export agency to the outside world for hard currency, or to puppet regimes for bartered goods, while the ruble was landlocked, enabled the government to subsidize the bread, energy, space exploration, nuclear arms, educational, cultural and sports organizations, and, in Western terms, a grossly inefficient economy. It allowed the closed society to become a belligerent superpower, at its demise in control of 400 million people. A group of intrepid politicians and economists, now within sight of an unprecedented, simultaneous turn to democracy and capitalism against great odds, deserves world sympathy, cooperation, and adequate financial aid to complete its mission.

* * *

There were no recognized budget deficits, as we account for them, in the former Soviet Russia, and apparently no unemployment. The great natural resources and hydroelectric projects loomed so large in world opinion that Gorbachev in his six-year period (1985–1991) borrowed or renewed about $60 billion from the world's leading banks and friendly countries. The general secretary, later president, was apparently unconcerned with the debt burden of scheduled payments, only with repairing the cash-flow deficits. Since the Soviet Union, unlike Central and South American and other post-World War II borrowers, had never defaulted on interest or principal, it was a favorite of the international banks, who now have the distinction of their own club, the London Club of burned creditors. The unpaid governments belong to the Paris Club.[4]

Gazprom and the Stock Market

If a moderate number of shares brings close to a half-billion, non-inflationary, non-printing press dollars, why not phase in the rest of the shares on the oversubscribed foreign market for at least $50 billion

4

more at the October 1996 sales price? Actually the world energy analysts figure that if Gazprom's reserves were valued at Western prices, and then marked down for Russia's political risk, the 100% market value would be at least in the $200 billion area, which is why the shares were snapped up. The successful underwriting represents a bet on Russia's economic recovery and on the ultimate restructuring of its biggest industrial corporation into a rationally-managed profit center.

The shares represent ownership in the world's largest natural gas producer. For all its inefficiency and old-style bureaucracy, its 1995 output was double that of the No. 2 producer, Royal Dutch-Shell Group, whose reserves are only one-thirtieth of Gazprom's. Gazprom has 375,000 employees and sells 21% of western Europe's gas through an endless pipeline from Siberia, bringing in about $27 billion annually, much of it hard currency from foreign sales.

Gazprom's privatization took place in mid-1994, towards the end of the great spin-off of state-owned enterprises that many believe pushed Russia permanently into the market system, regardless of continual political turmoil, sharply reduced gross domestic product and industrial production, and a majority of impoverished but vote-entitled citizens. These voters, incidentally, show up at the polls in far greater proportion than the increasingly disinterested electorates in the aging democracies. As a politically sensitive industrial dinosaur run by thousands of entrenched beneficiaries, Gazprom's newly-incorporated 23 billion shares were allocated for distribution by the privatization bureau as follows:

Government retained	40%
Russian investors	33%
Gazprom employees	15%
Treasury stock reserved for possible sale to foreigners	9%
Other	3%

Note that 40% is still owned by the government, hardly meriting the title privatization in capitalist terms. It is still a quasi-state enterprise, apparently enjoying tax exemptions, or at least decades of tax-paying

5

defiance, as an instrument of state policy. Russia has had its full of outside advisors, but a hypothetical question can be raised. Why not reduce government stock to 20% (the typical effective-control percentage in capitalist countries) and phase out 28%, including the remaining 8% foreign sale allotment, to the ready-for-bailout foreign investors, netting another $14 billion from this fortuitous asset? It would enable the government to pay pensions and other arrearages, rehabilitate and reduce its bloated 1.7 million army, always a political threat in times of economic trouble, and see light at the end of the tunnel. Nothing works so easily in Russia. Aside from the fact that the hard-nosed investment bankers would resist flooding the market with more shares than stipulated as reserved for foreigners, there are negative aspects of Gazprom as a capitalist enterprise.

Here the author can avoid charges that he is promoting Gazprom shares. It has yet to issue an audited financial statement, not needed in a command economy, so its profit or loss is still conjectural, although gross income is believed to be $27 billion, as noted. It needs at least $15 billion over the next decade for repairs and improvements, according to the bankers. We have noted it owed the government about $3 billion in delinquent taxes at the end of 1996, and the government is now serious about tax collection and revising its irrational tax code. Moreover, having entered the competitive capitalist market, subject to profit and loss restraints, and with no subsidies or captive customers, Gazprom must compete with Norway's Statoil, the second largest natural gas source for Western Europe, which announced in January 1997 a $14 billion contract over 25 years with Italian utilities. Norway's business plan is to double European sales by 1998. The irony of this role-reversal should not be lost on international energy executives, flying over targeted markets in nationalized airlines for the most part. Norway, still regarded as being in the capitalist camp, although consorting with socialism, is the 100% owner of Statoil. The point is not to condemn Russia's headlong plunge, but to keep in mind the ambiguities of an ideological rather than pragmatic attachment to market capitalism.

Interenterprise Arrearages

Returning to its role as a prototype for Russia's economic travails, Gazprom owed approximately $8 billion in "interenterprise payments," long overdue, in addition to its mammoth tax liability. For observers of transition economies, such payments represent a new category of economic dysfunction. The striking miners reported in the press, as many as 400,000 mainly in the Siberian regions at the end of 1996, are a good example. The coal operators, mostly private at this time, assert they cannot collect from their customers, the utilities, who in turn claim they cannot collect from the frazzled consumers, who feel energy should be plentiful and subsidized, as in the old days, especially in the cold Russian winters. This explanation is no doubt oversimplified for a highly complex issue unique to post-Cold War transition economies. Still the national total of arrearages, including unpaid military and state employee payrolls, as well as the interenterprise payments, is enormous, in the high double-digit billions, causing immense political and social unrest, as it should. Gazprom alone claims about $8 billion due from its utilities, as well as from defense industries and Russian Federation republics, who probably never intended to pay to start with.[5]

This absurd condition makes one speculate on the oft-proposed theory that Russian man, conditioned by generations of autocracy and collectivism before and during Communism, is not a candidate for "economic man," motivated by individual striving and the desire for gain to participate in an efficiency-driven market-system.[6] I do not give credence to this theory, believing that modern man, in a technological world of mass production and highly-promoted markets, will instinctively adjust his life to efficiency as a matter of necessity and common sense. What cannot be helped is the inertia, or vacuum, produced by seventy years of a command economy, without some gradual transition to new institutions, such as credit devices, inventory control, and enforceable contracts. Above all, Russia needs such capitalist standbys as bankruptcy for failed or redundant firms, employee layoffs and relocation, unemployment insurance and re-employment training, all devices that would alleviate, in this instance, the accumulation of interenterprise and other arrearages. If you are

7

going to have a market economy, why not adopt its built-in safety-valves and cushions? Perhaps it was impossible to do this under the pressure of circumstances, but the thought persists, six years later.

The Question of Management

A critical aspect of Russia's transition economy is the question of management. Who will run the privatized Gazprom, let alone the 18,000 other former state firms, from shoes to satellites, employing 100 or more people? Most of the old managers were Party members in good standing. They were not managers with memories of capitalism, as in Hungary, Poland, and Czechoslovakia, the neighboring success stories after the fall of the Berlin Wall in 1989, but third-generation bureaucrats, ministers, and plant superintendents, who had won their way to the top through merit and knowledge, as well as favoritism, without the discipline of profits and markets. They were motivated by status, power, and perks, and conditioned by a near-century of relentless propaganda about the injustices of capitalism.

The system was grossly inefficient by Western standards, but there is no gainsaying Russia's technical ability, its 100% literacy, avid readership,[7] and extremely high percentage of college, vocational and professional school graduates. Its armies engulfed Hitler's invasion, with 20 million military and civilian losses, but as tourists will recall, the state managed to rebuild its ravaged cities without foreign aid. In short, Russia's human capital is its other great natural resource, the factor many believe will push the chaotic country over the line to the comfort zones of capitalism as well as the freedom of democracy.

Still the lumbering managers and bureaucratic elites, disdainfully termed the *nomenklatura* by impatient reformers, have clogged the arteries of the economy, often deliberately, encouraged by nationalists and populists in the powerful Russian parliaments that emerged after the breakup of the Soviet Union and termination of the Party's power. It was Yeltsin's fate to skirmish continually with the military-industrial-populist complex in successive parliaments that denied him a majority at any time after the brief honeymoon in which he launched by presidential decrees his bold economic reforms.

8

The symbolic remedy to parliamentary and *nomenklatura* opposition was Viktor Chernomyrdin, the durable prime minister and present world figure who served as caretaker for the ailing Yeltsin. The image of Chernomyrdin is the familiar one of burly commissar in dark suit, with no-nonsense demeanor, unlike the smiling Yeltsin, who proved to be a born American-style politician. The two men had similar backgrounds. They knew each other from earlier careers in the remote Urals of Siberia, Yeltsin in Sverdlosk, Chernomyrdin in Orsk. Yeltsin, born in 1931 to a remarkably poor peasant family, a bright college graduate of the Urals Polytechnic, made his mark in the construction industry, became Party boss of Sverdlosk, Russia's fifth largest city, and forged ahead to Moscow on the basis of his administrative talent and reputation for integrity. Like Gorbachev, whose grandfather had been imprisoned for anti-Communist tendencies, his father narrowly escaped a similar arrest, a reminder of the validity of the suppressed commitment to democratic freedom on the part of both men. Gorbachev, of course, turned out to be lukewarm about radical economic reform, compared with his ebullient political rival Yeltsin.

Chernomyrdin, born in 1938, worked at the bottom in an oil refinery, graduated from a technical institute by way of a correspondence course, ultimately rose to be Soviet Minister of Gas, and then became the head of colossal Gazprom (1989–1992) before it was privatized, leaving to become Yeltsin's deputy prime minister in 1992. Observers of corporate management might concede that these two men, in an open capitalist environment, would have made it to the top in any advanced industrial country. They would be welcome contrasts to the get-rich-quick unsavory types flourishing in Russia's present interlude of predatory capitalism, an economic reality which may or many not have been a necessary consequence of a crash-type transition.

In his memoirs, Yeltsin reveals his empathy for the Gazprom impresario he appointed prime minister in December 1992 to replace the youthful Yegor Gaidar, repository of national anger for the hyperinflation and status shifts caused by the rapid economic reforms. Against signals from President Bush, demands from the international foreign aid emissaries, and advice from the non-Russian palace advisors attached to the Gaidar economic team, he made his choice:

9

. . . he was not a party worker but a manager in the state-run economy who had worked all over Siberia and the Ural Mountains region. He'd been through the school of hard knocks, and had seen the view not from the regional party offices but from the ground up. I had seen Chernomyrdin in swamp-waders up to his knees in mud - that was part of his job in the petroleum and gas-industry, and it was indeed a hard one.[8]

The powerful industrialist lived up to Yeltsin's expectations. He helped pacify the parliament, and surprised his critics, who saw him as an unabashed industrial lobbyist, by bringing in the highly effective and competent reformist Boris Federov as Russian finance minister for the critical year of 1993. Chernomyrdin also stood by Yeltsin during the inglorious but apparently justified shelling of parliament on October 4, 1993 after Yeltsin signed decree No. 1400 for its dissolution on September 21. The high number is an indication of the use of decrees, hundreds of which were ignored or subverted by the *nomenklatura* and their agents in parliament, by which Yeltsin managed to rule in the early days of reform, a Napoleon of decrees with insufficient authority. More to the point of economic reform, Chernomyrdin agreed to cashier Geraschenko, his favored central bank president, after Geraschenko in April 1993 opened the floodgates of printed money, the dreaded monetary-inflation bane of the reform professionals and foreign-aid mandarins from the International Monetary Fund and the World Bank.

Crony Capitalism

In its role as transition prototype, Gazprom can also be seen in terms of inside dealing between business interests and the state, an endemic affliction of modern capitalism whenever economic power attempts to cross the boundary lines separating business interests from government. A variation of crony capitalism was well-established in Soviet Russia, where well-connected insiders, often relatives of high-ranking politicians, became looters and embezzlers of state property and were often discovered and punished. Its continuation in Russia's tumultuous capitalism was inevitable. It is less deplorable than the rampant Mafia-like, gangster corruption that gravely undermines Russia's

10

present economic progress, to be examined later in this book, but it should be noted.

Reports abound that Chernomyrdin is a millionaire, perhaps several times over, from his Gazprom career, so far without substantiation. Anders Åslund, a world authority and on-the-scene participant in Russia's economic transition, states in a 1995 book:

> In 1994, Chernomyrdin became the dominant politician with regard to economic issues . . . He provided himself and his rent-seeking associates in the energy lobby with large illegitimate tax exemptions, making them the richest men in Russia.[9]

Rent-seeking is transition-jargon for manipulating industrial production items, such as siphoning off excess inventory to sham entities set up by the plant managers, or making a claim on resources of ambiguous ownership, or taking advantage of knowledge of impending scarcity created by a change in government policy.[10] It is not my intent to defend Chernomyrdin, who indeed may have enriched himself and his cronies by such skullduggery, varieties of which are amply reported in the transition literature. Recently, for example, Moscow-based reporters have described employees in small-arms factories engaged in daily, large-scale smuggling out of parts for assembly and resale, to eke out their living. The Mafia reportedly supplies the demand.

Chernomyrdin, for his part, symbolizes the obstructionist, bureaucratic manager intent on protecting his turf, whom Åslund excoriates repeatedly for stalling on reforms initiated by the professional advisors. It is understandable that these specialists, foreign and domestic, and international reporters as well, have their favorite villains, frequently the International Monetary Fund, whose austere loan conditions they hold responsible for Russia's alarming cash shortage.[11]

Staying with the $3 billion deferred or unpaid taxes owed by Gazprom in 1994, when it was still a subsidized operation rather than a tax-paying profit center, any improper gains in that area would have come not from tax exemptions but from outright embezzlement of state funds on a gigantic scale. This is something Chernomyrdin's many political opponents in Russia's multi-party parliament would hardly fail to raise. More likely his fortune came from Gazprom's going public.

* * *

Gazprom issued vouchers for 15% of its 23 billion shares to its 375,000 employees at giveaway prices, about 20¢ per share, a device intended to make a large segment of these employees instant capitalists, motivated to make and retain profits for themselves and their fellow shareholders. In addition, 33% of the shares were made available to the public. Every family in Russia had previously received vouchers worth about $80, which they could use to buy shares in privatized industries of their choice. It was anticipated that most of these vouchers would end up sold for cash or exchanged for shares in investment funds organized for this purpose. This in turn would produce funds, banks and other large holders with sufficient blocks of stock to exercise some effective control over management, a desirable capitalist strategy for such an epochal transformation of state enterprises into privatized enterprises. A voucher program along these lines had already worked reasonably well in the privatization programs of Poland and Czechoslovakia before Russia launched its own variation. As a result, Russia claims 40 million shareholders, through fund or personal shares, as proof of its capitalism.

Chernomyrdin left Gazprom to join the government before its privatization. Assuming he received a very substantial amount of shares in recognition of his former services, a practise quickly learned from the generous options and warrants that made immense fortunes for American computer and entertainment executives, and that he acquired with cash or loans considerably more through the voucher resale market, his Russian-based shares, acquired at about 40¢ or less would be worth at least five times as much two years later, based on the premium price paid by foreign buyers. This assumes that a seller's market exists, or would be allowed, since sales of Gazprom in Russia are presently highly restricted. Although a Stock Exchange now exists in Russia, and was something of a roaring success for intrepid investors in 1996, it still awaits the smoothly-functioning model of the advanced capitalist countries and their highly-regulated Exchanges. Suffice to say if Chernomyrdin acquired his shares on any less legitimate route, he would be charged with impermissible insider trading, in Western terms.

When we consider how a Western prime minister or president would have to divest, or completely divulge, such conflict-of-interest shares before taking office, we realize how successfully regulated capitalism, after much trial and error, has served all concerned in the stock market area, attracting the essential job-creating investment funds to the reassured capital market and its entrepreneurs, and to retirement funds as well.

* * *

In a book emphasizing the economic aspects of transition, Gazprom is a many-faceted paradigm. It is a clone of capitalism at its worst and at its possible best. On the political front, Russia has become a promising democracy, with active political parties, freedom of speech and press, fair elections, and constitutional separation of powers. Yeltsin grossly abused campaign ethics, accepting blatant business contributions and using state-controlled media to his advantage in 1996.[12] Still the referendum by which he boldly risked his presidency in 1993, and the two elections of 1996, show that the Russian people, despite their catastrophic reduction in living standards, voted against a return to the discredited time-warp of Communism, despite the blandishments of reactionary candidates such as the populist Zhirinovsky and the Communist Zyuganov. All the more reason for considering a final economic aberration displayed by Gazprom, its headlong rush into more monopoly. A state monopoly in the first place, and still owned 40% by the government, Gazprom bought in October 1996 20% of *Konsomolskaya Pravda*, one of Russia's most widely read newspapers, with a circulation of 1.6 million (see note 7). What other than political considerations would lead to such an acquisition? The company also owns 30% of NTV independent television and an undisclosed amount of Russian Television, two of the country's most popular networks. Finally, it recently announced it is seeking a 25% interest in Russia's electricity monopoly, United Energy Systems, a strategy management claims, with an eye on the company's stock-market price, that will enable it to gain a foothold in the nearby Asian energy market. For a company extraordinarily in debt, delinquent in billions of taxes, and already accounting for 9% of Russia's gross domestic product, these announcements from Gazprom's new skyscraper headquarters in Moscow indicate a conscious turn to oligarchic, not democratic, capitalism.

Similar acquisitions of valuable state properties, notably world leaders in oil and nickel, were made in the final 1996 stages of Russia's otherwise commendable privatization project, by banks and existing combines, along the lines of the cartels in Japan and South Korea, foreshadowing a Big Seven type of diversified financial-industrial groupings in Russia. The best one can say about this lurching evolution to capitalism from Communism is that the six-year period covered in this book (1992–1997) is still very fluid and subject to more unexpected consequences. The G-7 countries after all have their own varieties of capitalism, and our designated agents, the International Monetary Fund and the World Bank, are neither MacArthurs in control of a defeated military enemy nor enlightened Marshall Plan administrators of another time and place. For an analysis of what they are, and what they have done, we turn to the next chapter.

Notes

1 There are three indispensable accounts of the 1991–1995 economic transition period in Russia viewed as a whole. There are many other accounts by specialists, foreign and Russian, whose detailed books and articles on transition subdivisions, such as price and trade liberalization, financial and fiscal stabilization, and privatization, are most valuable.

Two of the three major accounts are written by world-class Russian experts, Sweden's Anders Åslund and Britain's Richard Layard, who were also palace advisors in or near the Kremlin for an important part of this epochal period. A third world-class expert, Marshall Goldman, Harvard's Sovietologist, was not invited to the reform birth-pangs, perhaps to his dismay, but his account accordingly is free from self-justification about failed or stalled policies.

The bias of these books is revealed by their titles. (See Anders Åslund: *How Russia Became a Market Economy* (Washington, DC: Brookings Institution, 1995); Richard Layard and John Parker, *The Coming Russian Boom: A Guide to New Markets and Politics* (New York: The Free Press, 1996); and Marshall Goldman, *Lost Opportunity: Why Economic Reforms in Russia Have Not Worked* (New York: Norton, 1994). In his 1996 revision, Goldman backtracks somewhat, offering a new subtitle: *Lost Opportunity: What Has Made Russian Reform So Difficult?*, but he is still a dissenter, especially on social costs and foreign aid.

To these accounts must be added the reporting of major journalists, continuing at a high level, particularly in the *New York Times*, *Washington Post*, *Los Angeles Times*, *Wall Street Journal*, and Britain's *The Economist*, whose John Parker has reported on Russia since 1989, and who co-authored Layard's book. Of great distinction stands David Remnick (see *Lenin's Tomb, The Last Days of the Soviet Empire*, New York: Random House, 1993, and his subsequent articles in *The New Yorker*, *Foreign Affairs*, and *New York Review of Books*). On assignment from the *Washington Post* to Moscow in January 1988, accompanied by his new young wife, he stayed there to witness the bizarre putsch of August 1991 against Gorbachev that doomed the Soviet empire. Trusted and accepted by intellectuals, journalists, generals, and politicians of all stripes, he produced a narrative that justly won a Pulitzer prize. Hedrick Smith's *The New Russians* (see updated version, New York, 1993), is strong on the early Gorbachev era, complementing Remnick.

One must not forget this was primarily a political revolution. The march to capitalism, however pleasing to capitalists, was a secondary goal, constantly restrained by political figures and circumstances. Gorbachev has weighed in with a lengthy tome, but Yeltsin's candid, human memoirs (see *The Struggle for Russia*, New York: Times Books, 1994), based partly on his diaries, is one of the most unusual books ever written by a world politician while in office.

2 Alexander Livshits, Yeltsin's scholarly Finance Minister, announced in February 1997 Russian plans to sell $2 to $5 billion additional international bonds on various markets, starting with a deutschemark issue. Asked about his Jewish name in an interview with the *RUSSIAN* magazine in June 1996, he answered if that comes up, he'll gladly use a

15

pseudonym, "Call me Rabinowich," indicating progress on that Russian problem. Russian cities are also attracting bond investors, domestic and foreign. Moscow, which calls itself the world's busiest construction site, launched its own $400 million high-rate Eurobond issue in March 1997. (*Wall Street Journal*, 6 March 1997, A-10.)

3 Russia's budget deficits as a per cent of gross domestic product, after Yeltsin's takeover:

1991	1992	1993	1994	1995	1996	1997
20	18.8	8	10	4.3	7.7	(see note below)

Source: Mainly from IMF and World Bank publications, the most reliable available.

Note: During the Soviet Union period, budgets were not announced or published. The 1997 budget calls for a deficit goal of approximately 4% ($15 billion). For comparison, note that to join or maintain membership in the European Union, a country's budget deficit as per cent of gross domestic product must not exceed 3%. The US deficit is currently about 2% of its gross domestic product.

* * *

Average annual rate of inflation in Russia:

1991	1992	1993	1994	1995	1996	1997 (Est.)*
5.6	92.7	1,353	896	303	190	10–15

Source: For 1991–1996, World Bank, *From Plan to Market*, 1996, table A.3, 174.

*Russia claims its 1997 rate is down to 2% to 4% monthly. But after six years of cumulative inflation, the 1991 ruble is practically worthless.

4 Soviet debt to Western banks, assumed by Russia after Yeltsin's takeover, as of January 1, 1994:

Commercial Banks (The London Club)	$ billions
German	6.25
Italian	4.02
French	2.11
Austrian	1.22
American	1.22
Total	14.82

Soviet debt to Western countries, assumed by Russia after Yeltsin's takeover as of January 1, 1994:

Countries (The Paris Club)	$ billions
Germany	15.90
Italy	5.22
United States	2.72
France	2.58
Austria	1.82
Total	28.24

Source: Selected from Åslund, *How Russia Became a Market Economy*, 1995, 283, whose source is his own Institute for Economic Analysis, based on figures from the Russian Ministry of Finance.

The burned banks are loath to reveal their identities, content with the capitalist reward for risk-takers, bad-debt deductions on their income tax and some prospects for long-term recovery. Practically all of the above debts have been generously reconstructed or settled for deferred payment without any near-term burden for Russia, which assumed the debts only as a good-will gesture after the takeover. Of great significance is what a powerhouse Germany proved to be, extending $22 billion of the above $43 billion to its former enemy. Also how circumspect Thatcher's Britain was, and how trusting Italy.

17

5   Interenterprise arrearages are controversial. Åslund and Layard claim they have been grossly exaggerated. They never existed in the Soviet system, so their appearance reflects the change to a market system, in which normal billing-time would cut the total figure by at least half. Also since many firms are both creditors and debtors, only the net amount owed should be considered in the total. They say the bureaucrats are to blame, shipping without credit precautions or firm orders, or running up arrearages in expectation of a government bailout. Others claim it is a "money crunch" problem, with the International Monetary Fund, because of its government budget and credit restraints as conditions for its loans, to blame. A striking coal-miner might reply, paraphrasing Zhivago to Strelnikov: "Your explanation. My hunger."

6   Debate over the particularism of the Russian psyche can get out of hand. It centers on a disposition to collective passivity, interrupted by violent revolution or terrorism, led by Utopians. This is at odds with the vision of capitalism's pragmatic merchants, gradually outwitting and overcoming the restraints of feudalism and monarchy. But Yeltsin's troubles may have more to do with predatory, unregulated capitalists than with capitalism's instinct for property, profit, law, and order. (See Tim McDaniel: *Agony of the Russian Idea*, Princeton, 1996, for the exclusivity argument, and Layard, *Coming Russian Boom*, 1996, 7-94, for the "makes no difference" reply.)

7   Newspaper circulation in Russia is problematical. David Remnick reports in 1990–91, the time of transition from Gorbachev to Yeltsin, these leaders: *Argumenti i Fakti*, 30 million, and *Konsomolskaya Pravda*, 25 million (*Lenin's Tomb*, 1993, 376). Considering the "official" *Pravda* was acknowledged by the West to be a technological triumph of slanted news to about 11 million, compared with America's circulation front-runner, the *Wall Street Journal* with 1.9 million, could Remnick be wrong? Greta Adamova, Managing Editor of the *RUSSIAN* magazine (US), checked in Moscow in March 1997 at my request and supplied these figures (millions):

	1984		1997
Trud (the labor paper)	15.4	*Argumenti i Fakti*	3.4
Konsomolskaya Pravda	11.3	*Konsomolskaya Pravda*	1.6
Pravda	10.4	(several others smaller; Moscow	
Izvestia	6.4	has about 25 newspapers)	

18

Ms. Adamova was a schoolteacher in Russia for many years. About 2 of her 200 ruble monthly salary went for journals, especially those politically correct. Payments were made at the 20,000 neighborhood banks of the old system. The 1984 circulation covered the republics of the former Soviet Union. With capitalism will come an Audit Bureau of Circulation.

8 Yeltsin, *The Struggle for Russia*, 1994, 199.

9 Åslund, *How Russia Became a Market Economy*, 1995, 315.

10 World Bank, *From Plan to Market*, 1996, viii.

11 Richard Boudreaux, *Los Angeles Times*, 4 December 1996, "Russians Strike, Demanding Unpaid Wages," A–11. He states: "Russia's cash crisis stems from sharp government curbs on the money supply, prescribed by the International Monetary Fund to wipe out inflation." In response to my inquiries, IMF refuses to accept all or part of the blame, referring to "interenterprise arrearages." (See IMF Occasional Paper No. 133, 1995, Chapters 4 and 8, for the IMF position.)

12 Remnick, *New Yorker*, 22 July 1996, "The War for the Kremlin," 40–58; also Daniel Treisman, "Why Yeltsin Won," *Foreign Affairs*, Sept. Oct. 1996, 64–77.

2 Western Aid: The International Monetary Fund

At the end of 1996, President Yeltsin could contemplate a third economic bonanza, which established a foundation for the unexpected Eurobond and Gazprom successes. This was the great generosity and good sense of the Western nations, through their agency, the International Monetary Fund, in granting $6.8 billion aid to Russia in April 1995, and an additional $10.1 billion in April 1996. After three years of too little, too late, and much recrimination on both sides, the anemic 1991–94 grants of $4 billion were redeemed by a munificent $16.9 billion windfall. There was no dancing in the streets in Russia upon the news. This was not outright humanitarian aid for its new poverty class. It included more hard-nosed, professional foreign aid intended to end Russia's murderous inflation and restore its battered industrial production, by way of continued market-oriented reforms guaranteed to hurt as well as heal. It was, however, also clearly directed at quick social relief. Since the average Russian has as little understanding as the average American about IMF, the following review will help establish its role in Russia's march to capitalism. We can then assess what IMF is and what it has accomplished.

A Review of International Monetary Fund Aid to Russia

The period is from Yeltsin's takeover after the aborted coup against Gorbachev on September 19–21, 1991 through 1996.

Background: Russia, as survivor of the former Soviet Union

20

empire, becomes a member of IMF in April 1992, paying in $4.5 billion to join the club. Yeltsin and his economic reform chief, Yegor Gaidar, backed by behind-the-scenes strategists Jeffrey Sachs of Harvard and Sweden's Anders Åslund, seek recognition and massive funds from Western countries, after launching their "radical reform" transition from socialism to a market economy on January 2, 1992 with an overnight freeing of most regulated prices, a calculated invitation to inflation, which they hope will be for the short run.

* * *

First Period: Too little, too late. IMF unprepared to press for Russia's needs as Western governments dawdle.

Year	Amount Authorized ($ billions)	Amount Distributed through 1996
1992 (July)	1.0	1.0

IMF hesitantly grants $1 billion, available January 1993. Yeltsin goes with begging bowl to G-7 nations. Gets unfulfilled and unrealistic promises from G-7 finance ministers of $25 billion in quick aid on April 6, 1992 and an equally spurious promise of $28 billion on April 3, 1993. A proposed IMF $6 billion currency stabilization fund is abandoned.

* * *

Second Period: Mutual recrimination.

Year	Amount Authorized ($ billions)	Amount Distributed through 1996
1993 (April)	1.5	1.5
1994 (April)	1.5	1.5
	3.0	3.0

Starting here, it is understood Russia can use IMF money for general budget relief, a departure from IMF's traditional function of financing trade deficits, subject to compliance with IMF's anti-inflationary goals, involving decreased government spending and painful reduction of budget deficits. IMF becomes furious at Russia's billion dollar bailout of wages, pensions and intercompany payment arrearages in 1993, and billions more spent on a failed attempt to stop a ruble plunge in 1994. Meanwhile, hyperinflation has rocked Russia and Yeltsin has to face revolt by shelling his own parliament on October 4, 1993. Yeltsin has sacked Gaidar and replaced him with Chernomyrdin, but by mid-1994 Russia has irretrievably lurched to a democratic market society, although one racked by corruption and questionable social costs.

The point of no return: three-quarters of Russian industry has been privatized.

* * *

Third Period: IMF redeems itself (and the West) with a massive aid program of $16.9 billion, a totally new ball-game for Russia.

Year	Amount Authorized ($ billions)	Amount Distributed through 1996
1995 (April)	6.8	6.8
1996 (April)	10.1	2.7
	16.9	9.5
Total	20.9	13.5

IMF, following the political wishes of its G-7 controlling owners (US: 18.25%), comes up with two important decisions. First, it will pay out the 1995–96 $16.9 billion in monthly installments, prodding compliance by stopping payments rather than harangue a sovereign member-nation *ex-post facto*. The 1995 money has been distributed in full. The 1996 payments ($340 million monthly over 36 months) were stopped in October 1996 for several months until Russia cracked down on income tax evasion. Second, in its role as team-leader for World

Bank and other aid institutions, IMF places key staff members constantly in Russia rather than Washington. Its stamp of approval supports Russia's 1996 crucial entry into the Eurobond market and the initial public offering of Russia's crown jewel, Gazprom, to foreigners.

* * *

Summary: IMF lent Russia $13.5 billion in the critical five years (1992–96) following Yeltsin's commitment to democracy and capitalism. The grand total in 1998 will be $20.9 billion. Russia has paid back $500,000 on the 1992 advance along with nominal interest as scheduled. Considering Russia paid in $4.5 billion to join the club, it can still default and come out $16 billion ahead, so IMF has taken a risk. IMF can easily absorb the loss, and the post-Cold War world can stand the benefits. An understanding of the leading and controversial role of IMF is essential for analyzing the role of the West in the great transition.

What is the IMF?

How does a strangely-named institution, founded by Americans, headquartered in Washington, and traditionally headed by a Frenchman, lend a potential $20.9 billion to Russia over six years, or for that matter, authorize $17 billion at one stroke to Mexico in 1995?

Before exploring origins, one must note that IMF aid for Russia did not have to run the gauntlet of Congress, where inevitably it would have engendered acrimonious debate and compromise. Although it monitors Russia's budget expenditures in detail, from government subsidies to the funding of reckless campaign promises, IMF escapes the scrutiny of US deficit hawks, since no taxpayers' money is currently involved. IMF steps into the breach for an America that has presided over a steady decline in foreign-aid expenditure, including its own State Department expense and United Nations membership fees. American foreign aid currently runs at an embarrassing 1% of annual budget, far below Germany and Japan measured by the same ratio. President Bush, for his part, was quite satisfied with the Nobel Peace

Prize-winning Gorbachev, having met with him in Moscow only days before the attempted coup. Fresh from offering his own begging bowl to G-7 nations for financing the Persian Gulf War, Bush was not prepared to shower funds on the upstart Yeltsin, either through Congress or the IMF. The Marshall Plan after World War II, for comparison, was a lofty, bipartisan, political-economic enterprise of a prosperous, victorious nation, hardly aware of the recently-created IMF.

* * *

The Great Depression of the 30s was aggravated by international money problems that devastated trade among nations. In addition to highly visible bank failures, farm prices below cost of production, and empty smokestacks everywhere, foreign trade fleets languished in harbors without cargoes. A widespread fear of paper money led to a demand for gold that national treasuries could not supply. For years the gold standard system had defined currencies in terms of their value for an ounce of gold, giving foreign trade contracts a known and stable value, but England and then America abandoned the gold standard as no longer feasible. A new international monetary exchange system was needed, with a new institution to monitor it, for trade or even tourism to flourish. It would see to it that currencies were readily convertible into each other on a reliable basis.

J.M. Keynes, the British economist famed for advocating the end of depression through state intervention, and Harry Dexter White, a US Treasury official later to become a target of Senator Joseph McCarthy, advanced proposals for such an agency in the early 40s. They were barely noticed as the drums of war rumbled. Negotiations among 44 nations at Bretton Woods, New Hampshire, anticipating the end of the war, finally created the IMF, to be started in Washington in 1946. Its 39 members have now become 181.

It is helpful to regard IMF not as a bank but as a giant cooperative, owned by its trading members of all sizes, who contribute a substantial quota, according to size, to join the club. Each member is entitled to draw within limits on the combined pool of money for the primary purpose of financing trade deficits, when they need temporary help with such payments. Example: Country A imports $1 billion more than it exports to B. Country A needs $1 billion yen, available from its central bank, for its importers to pay B. The central bank does not have sufficient foreign payment reserves in its treasury, so it draws on IMF, repaying IMF when its reserves and the country's balance of trade are more favorable. The IMF does not issue yen, but its own currency, called SDR's, or Special Drawing Rights, based on an amalgam of five leading currencies (dollar, yen, mark, pound, and franc), presently worth about $1.40 per SDR. The SDR's are fully convertible as needed for any member's currency.

Much anguish can result from such a reductive explanation, typical of an American whose country doesn't need or use IMF financing. IMF's leading customers have been Mexico, UK, Argentina, India, Russia and Brazil, in that order, for the 1947–1995 period. Its quotas now amount to $210 billion. It has 2,600 employees, the most skilled financial analysts and statisticians in the world, although many prefer to be on the Beltway rather than on assignment. It pumped billions of dollars into the foreign trade system during the debt crisis of member countries in the 80s, billions to Mexico, and now billions to Russia and the other transition economies. Above all it monitors and reviews the economic performance of every member and transmits the reviews with suggestions on how to remedy economic weaknesses. It insists that member countries notify IMF of any changes, such as intent to devalue their currencies, that could hurt other countries. IMF members use a variety of methods to determine the exchange value of their currencies, some pegged to the dollar, some to the franc, but most of them pegged to flexible standards, requiring constant monitoring. Above all IMF is "the enemy of surprise," somewhat diminished by the total surprise of the Mexican crisis. "Surveillance" is the new IMF watchword, and the agency has announced plans to establish a supplementary credit line of about $28 billion to avert another Mexican fiasco. Also, quotas may have to be raised, affecting the US, with 18.25% of total quotas, and Germany, Japan, France, and UK, with about 5% each. Since quotas determine the relative weight of votes on decisions such as aid to Russia, this 40% bloc represents effective control by the Western countries.

25

The Mexican Crisis Comparison

The Mexican crisis can be reviewed for two reasons. First, it illustrates the fragility of today's global, unregulated capitalism, marked by instant, massive transfers of money, usually to higher rates, or sudden demands for immediate repayment, subject to no loyalty other than the desire for speculative profit or the fear of further loss. These unregulated transfers can jeopardize national debt-financing programs and they inhibit domestic policies seeking to restrain inflation and promote growth. Ironically, innovative capitalism, in its time of triumph over socialist gridlock, is confronted with the ubiquitous chip, which may require a new order of responsibilities for an agency like the IMF. Second, the IMF Mexican operation, though unusual, differs greatly from the major change of policy designed expressly for Russia.

* * *

Briefly, Mexico, lulled by the euphoria of expansion, had financed its trade and budget deficits by relying heavily on an unprecedented number of anonymous, short-term, investors throughout the world, who could withdraw their money instantly, but were glad to renew their profitable investments in a surging country "too large to fail." A crisis of confidence occurred in 1994 when the peso was devalued, typically a strategy to boost a country's exports by lowering the price of its products to foreign buyers. When Mexico belatedly announced it might default on short-term borrowings if redemption demands continued to accelerate, the plug was pulled and investors, both foreign and domestic, withdrew billions of dollars from Mexico in a state of panic. An analogy can be found in the American savings and loan crisis of the late 80s, when irresponsible executives and their boards of directors, gloating over the deregulation that allowed conservative home-mortgage institutions to profiteer in any venture they could get their hands on, canvassed the world for high-rate short-term deposits, in this case guaranteed by federal insurance. When the bubble of bad loans burst and the S&L's failed, American taxpayers had to finance the bailout as the FDIC paid out hundreds of billions to depositors. The scandal exacerbated America's budget deficits, at a record high largely due to arming against Russia, and dampened its capacity for worthy endeavors of democratic capitalism, including foreign aid to a peaceful Russia.

Enough time has passed to evaluate the Mexican crisis, which was as short in duration as Russia's has been long. The $50 billion package originally deemed necessary to prevent Mexican bankruptcy, and also to allay the spread of similar crises to emerging countries throughout the world, was exaggerated. The total actually distributed was only $12.5 billion of the IMF $17 billion standby credit, and a $13.5 billion five-year loan from the US, a total of $26.0 billion. The US came into the picture partially because the IMF's institutional limit is roughly three times a member's quota. Treasury Secretary Robert Rubin, a sophisticated Wall Street veteran, aware of the importance of Mexican trade with the US, discovered funds previously authorized for such an emergency, easing the Congressional obstacle. Additionally, the US loan was secured by a lien on Mexico's national oil reserves, a claim which could hardly be exercised but which propped up the loan. Unspoken was the fact that a country with a 2,000-mile border with Mexico might be overwhelmed by illegal emigrants without hope of work at home, illustrating the geopolitical aspects of foreign aid.

The good news is that in January 1997 Mexico repaid the US the last $3.5 billion of its loan, three years ahead of time, with a ceremony resembling a successful peace treaty. IMF has been paid back $3.3 billion of its $12.5 billion, and is on its way to advance payment in full. Where did the money come from? In August 1996 J.P. Morgan Securities Ltd led a group underwriting $6 billion of Mexican Notes maturing in 2001 and Mexico is busy obtaining even longer-term debt on the various world bond markets. Market capitalists came to the rescue after government intervention prepared the way.

The bad news is that the harsh IMF prescription, involving higher interest rates on domestic loans, sharp tax increases, government spending cuts, and an unrelieved cash shortage, created a deep recession in 1995. More than 1 million Mexicans lost their jobs, and paychecks were devastated by soaring prices. Now the economy has revived, and there is some worry that the battered peso may go too high, affecting Mexican exports in the high-stakes world of global trade and finance. Given that world, one should hesitate before bashing government regulatory institutions.

How Russian and Mexican IMF Aid Differ

The similarity in size and contemporaneity has been noted. A first difference is in the loan structure. The Mexican advance was a typical IMF standby loan, available for a one-year period and requiring a short-term payback. The key $10.1 billion portion of the Russian loans of 1995–1996 is payable over 4 to 10 years, and the initial payments are substantially deferred, a rare long-term payment program for IMF. The Mexican loan was related to a threat of national bankruptcy, which might ground Mexico as a world-trading partner. Matched by funds from the US, it was a signal to the world's creditors that Mexico's debts would be repaid and that its central bank reserves had been restored after the major capital outflows in late 1994. This is reasonably related to IMF's charter to remedy trade-deficit payment problems. In Russia's case, trade deficits were not a major concern, and there was no need to reassure the world's creditors about Russia's repayment of the $80 billion owed to creditors of the defunct Soviet Union, which Russia had so casually assumed in the days after the putsch. The new country, and its new president, soon made it clear that these loans had best be forgotten or written off, while the historic turn to democracy and the market system took priority for any foreign aid available.

The question remains, what basis existed for the special nature of IMF's Russian loans? As noted in the history of such loans at the beginning of this chapter, in April 1993 it was recognized that Russia could use new IMF money for general budget relief, a departure from IMF's traditional function of financing trade deficits. True, IMF loan conditions sought to channel its funds towards reform of the discredited system rather than allow inflationary budget-deficit spending. Its method generally was to hector the sovereign member-nation in that direction after the damage was done. This period of mutual recrimination was solved with the 1995–96 $19.6 billion package, whose remaining $340 million monthly payments are doled out subject to withholding if either government spending or sabotage of reforms gets too far out of line.

A combination of IMF bureaucratic insight, enlightened G-7 political pressure, and plain stubbornness on the part of the harassed

Yeltsin and his advisory economists, resulted in a policy adjustment of historic significance. IMF now acknowledges that the current Russian advances are in fact direct loans that can be largely used for budget relief, the most generous form of foreign aid, or at least that they produce the same effect.

Evaluating IMF Aid

There would be no point in defending IMF aid to Russia if there were not substantial criticism. Leading the attack would be Jeffrey Sachs, the Harvard professor and world authority on economic advice to transition countries, from Russia to China, who will be discussed in chapter 4. "The IMF is an extremely mediocre institution," Sachs recently stated to the *Wall Street Journal*, remembering his early Russian experience and commenting on the agency's plans to increase surveillance and raise more money, "nobody should be fooled that this is under control."[1] Vice President Al Gore has spoken of IMF's "too much shock, not enough therapy" for Russia. Walter Russell Mead repeats the question: "Is fifty years enough?" in *Foreign Affairs*.[2]

Marshall Goldman has reservations about IMF's imposition of harsh remedies without sufficient authority. At the same time, he criticizes foreign advisors like Sachs and Åslund, who he believes have a vested interest in their reforms and wanted unlimited IMF funds to insure results.[3] Goldman is more convincing in other areas of his criticism of Russian reform, such as failure to build market institutions, excessive shock treatment, and the terrible social costs involved.

Another verdict comes from Richard Layard, one of the distinguished foreign economic advisors who joined the Gaidar team in November 1991 and, like Sachs and Åslund, was intimately involved with the economic transition, spending roughly half his time in Moscow in the early years, away from his professorship at the London School of Economics. Like the other palace advisors, he is sharply critical of some IMF programs, such as the determined effort to maintain a central ruble zone for the newly-independent states after the breakup of the Soviet Union. Under the proposed IMF plan, fortified

29

by guest appearances of European Union officials dedicated to one currency for all its members, the states' central banks would continue to issue rubles independently. This would make Russia's assets subject to raids at bargain prices, the advisors protested, assuming the likely prospect that a neighbor's ruble might become even more inflated than the Russian ruble. Layard graphically describes this situation as "the curse of the ruble zone," reflecting heated economic passions, tumultuous at the time, but now only a blip on the IMF ledger.[4] In retrospect, Layard concludes:

> People sometimes say that the IMF dictated conditions to Russia that were contrary to its interests. The reverse is true. In most cases the reformers wanted the IMF to impose the conditions in order to strengthen the reformers' hands within the government. The IMF did not dictate; it provided important intellectual support in thinking systematically about what needed to be done . . . While an early proactive policy from the G-7 would have been far better [at the start], even then things would have been worse still without the IMF.[5]

* * *

In all fairness, IMF did not seek the leadership role of Western aid to Russia. It inherited it by default. The ending of the Cold War justified attention from representatives at the highest cabinet level of the G-7 countries, not just finance ministers and globally-preoccupied bureaucratic institutions, especially on the basic policy concepts of how much democracy and how much market system should be sought at the start and down the road, as well as how the various aid sources should be coordinated. It was primarily a political matter, without political leadership.

* * *

My own bias, as must be apparent, is to deplore mindless enshrinement of laissez-faire market ideology over the pragmatic regulation of capitalism in the democratic state. Such regulation is now widely under attack, sometimes with good reason, by advocates of growth

30

and efficiency. IMF's classic transition reform-strategies of overnight price liberalization, budget and spending controls, convertible currency, privatization of state property, and elimination of government subsidies and restrictions, may sound like an adventure in Hayek-land, but is that really the issue? The program in context can be seen as an effort to shed the illiberal straitjacket of economic socialism rather than intentionally ignore the safeguards and social justice of advanced capitalism. As noted, the latter takes time and has its own variations reflecting national traditions and even ethnicity. Perhaps to get to step B, especially in fossilized Russia, only a radical break with the past, and much resulting pain, could be contemplated. When Russia's pain reached the breaking point, however, Western foreign aid wisely turned to direct budget relief.

Notes

1 *Wall Street Journal*, 31 December 1996, A-4.

2 *Foreign Affairs*, January/February 1997, 146.

3 Goldman, *Lost Opportunity*, 223–24.

4 Layard, *The Coming Russian Boom*, 75–7; Åslund, *How Russia Became a Market Economy*, 109–33; David Lipton and Jeffrey D. Sachs, "Prospects for Russia's Economic Reforms," *Brookings Papers on Economic Activity*, no. 2, 1992, 237.

5 Layard, *The Coming Russian Boom*, 93.

3 The World Bank and Other Aid to Russia

The World Bank

The World Bank, like IMF founded in Bretton Woods, New Hampshire, at the close of World War II, has also grown prodigiously. Its 44 nations have become 180, and are basically the same for the two institutions. Both agencies were scorned from the start by the Soviet Union as capitalist threats, but the empire's successor nations have become members in good standing.

Together these organizations claim to be twin pillars supporting the structure of the world's economic and financial order. In retrospect they were a product of the unprecedented world economic disorder of the Great Depression preceding World War II, which at least has not been repeated. Their vision was also inspired by post-war dreams of prosperity and well-being for all nations, still painfully elusive as the world divides itself into rich and poor nations, probing daily into each other's lives through a new source of envy, omnipresent TV. There is on balance worldwide approval for the largesse of these immense agencies, subject to occasional critical analysis as in this book, and currently from prominent journalists, drawn to the debate by the harsh travails of the Russian transition. The general approval indicates that economic organizations enjoy a far better reception than a supra-government institution such as the United Nations, mired by rival political alignments and also veering toward rich and poor camps. For a new world order as the millennium approaches, the economy is becoming paramount, as it has already become for the leading post-Cold War nations.

For the transition countries, there is an important distinction to make between the two agencies. The IMF, for all its free-market talk, can also be seen as ideologically neutral, aside from its open-trade antecedents. Its self-perception is that of a master-central bank, seeking financial responsibility from its clients. Accordingly, it relies on currency convertibility, budget restraints, elimination of subsidies, fighting inflation, and similar financial devices as the best formula on hand for the abolition of command socialism, which the transition countries, other than China, have democratically voted to accomplish. Social implications are recognized but not given priority.

The World Bank, by charter humanitarian and by tradition presided over by an American, is concerned with giving the world's poorest nations a leg up on the development ladder. It has literally showered billions of dollars on the weakest nations, averting a banker's eye on probable repayment. Its 10,100 employees, headquartered in Washington, with forty offices throughout the world, constitute a massive arsenal of international technocrats: engineers, urban planners, agronomists, and environmentalists, as well as experts in telecommunications, water supply, population, health care, and similar disciplines.

Over 75% of its $300 billion expended to date has been for projects related to roads, dams, power stations, bridges, agricultural development, and similar infrastructure for economic growth. It also spends about $1 billion a year giving technical advice on these projects, training the receiving country for takeover. It has had notable successes, but also substantial failures. Often cited is a major road through the Amazon rain forest, funded in the 80s, that attracted tens of thousands of migrants who razed trees, exhausted the soil, and spread deadly epidemics among the hapless residents. It is still a negative venture.

The Bank's major lending agency is accurately named the International Bank for Reconstruction and Development. Over twenty countries have graduated from IBRD loans. Japan, for example, borrowed large sums for over a decade. Now it is one of the major lenders to World Bank, which unlike IMF readily raises the money it needs through worldwide sale of its bonds, appropriately rated AAA because of the sponsor's pedigree. It is capitalized at $182 billion by the world's leading countries, including a $5.4 billion subscription by Russia, of which only a nominal $334 million was required to be paid-in.[1]

* * *

China, incidentally, has long been an active member of the World Bank's transition group, enjoying a remarkable status in the sometimes apolitical world of foreign aid. The World Bank divides its member countries into income categories according to gross domestic product per capita. By the time China's 1.3 billion population is divided into its burgeoning GDP, the great new threat to capitalism comes out in the lowest bracket of all, $725 or less per capita, qualifying for the most generous and lowest-rate loans, while getting high grades from the World Bank on its fabulous progress. Foreign aid to China, mostly from the World Bank, has averaged about $3 billion yearly from 1990 through 1995. This is more than double the Bank's $6.4 billion to Russia through 1996.[2] India, Mexico and China receive the most World Bank aid in that order.

The Bank's Ideology

Free-market ideology was not a factor in the Bank's early days of participation in the Marshall Plan, conceived by Secretary of State George C. Marshall, launched by President Truman, and administered by the politically-empowered Paul G. Hoffman. This unprecedented foreign aid combined a victor's magnaminity with a policy of containing Russian influence in Europe, as well as providing a major market for trade exports to Europe, especially from America.

A major shift in policy was inaugurated by James D. McNamara, the Vietnam War Defense Secretary, whose resignation under fire was rewarded by President Johnson with the prestigious World Bank presidency. In his thirteen years at the post (1968–81), McNamara turned the bland agency into a powerhouse of activity, demanding more and more projects to alleviate poverty as a measure for career

34

advancement among the Bank's revitalized bureaucracy. Many believe McNamara's epic endeavor was a moral response to his Vietnam dilemma, resulting in casual disregard for prevailing political and economic systems in recipient countries.[3]

By the time investment banker James D. Wolfensohn took over in June 1995, a strong element of free-market ideology, in keeping with the Thatcher-Reagan heritage, had entered World Bank literature and program objectives. The unimpeded market-system is strongly advocated not only as consistent with democracy, but also as the only feasible alternative for even the poorest of nations to develop resources and eventually prosper. On the other hand, the present Bank administration, recognizing the shattering impact of reform-related social displacement in Russia, announced in April 1997 an unexpected $3 billion loan to promote social relief, full-steam ahead for 1997. The money will be used to support low-income citizens as well as overhaul the pension system, pay child-care allowances, and carry out housing and energy-savings projects. President Wolfensohn made the announcement in a meeting with Boris Nemtsov, the popular, independent thirty-seven-year-old former regional governor recently recruited by Yeltsin as first-deputy prime minister to give a new face to his cabinet. Also announced was an additional World Bank loan of $3 billion to finance housing and utilities reform, indicating Wolfensohn may tangle with the so-far impregnable Gazprom, the tax-evading energy monopoly, on behalf of Russia's least-advantaged.

This $6 billion supplement to IMF's recent billions, also aimed at Russia's budget relief, creates a total of $27 billion originated by the two agencies since mid-1995. Hopefully, the total cash injections will not be too late for Russia at the brink, regardless of which transition strategies, shock therapy, predatory capitalism, or political stasis, are held to blame. Social relief is a far cry from the Bank's traditional emphasis on items like roads, dams, and hydroelectric facilities, but then Russia is an emergency case, with previously demonstrated competence of its own in those areas. Here is Michael Carter, Director of World Bank's Moscow office, setting the stage for the change:

One of the biggest results of Russia's transition towards a market economy has been a growing incidence of poverty among its population.

In 1996, 32 million people [out of 148 million] were classified as living below the poverty line while many other households experienced financial insecurity because of late payment of public sector wages and pensions. The World Bank believes that Russia must engineer a strong but effective safety-net to move people out of poverty and to ease social tensions at a time when the country needs to push ahead with greater structural reforms.[4]

A $6 billion contribution directed towards economic victims at the expense of market efficiency does not in itself constitute a major policy shift for the far-flung Bank, which lends worldwide $20 billion annually, but it does testify to the vulnerability of ideology, always at risk when times and conditions reach a breaking point.

For Mr. Wolfensohn, bureaucracy, not ideology, remains his major problem at the World Bank. He has challenged his thousands of entrenched PhD's to stop their conference-jargon ("no more mention of Gini-coefficients!")[5], cut the tedious reviews of proposals on the way to final approval, and dispatched upper-level personnel out of Washington to spend more hands-on time in client countries.[6] He is sensitive to criticism from the left, that the Bank is a capitalist tool, and from the right, that there is less and less need for World Bank projects, and their embarrassing rate of successful completion, when foreign investment for emerging and transition countries is at a record level. Why not contract with private firms, with possibly a loss-guarantee for the riskiest countries? Finally, there is the lurking charge, in an age of merger mania, that the IMF and World Bank should be consolidated and downsized to eliminate needless duplication.[7]

The Coal Industry Fiasco

A case history of World Bank's good intentions gone awry can be found in its recent $525 million project for Russia's ailing coal industry. For years, the plight of coal miners, mostly in the remote northern regions, with as many as 400,000 clamoring for back pay, has made worldwide news. As noted in chapter 1, the coal mines, a majority now privatized, were caught up in a maze of "interenterprise arrearages," unable to collect from their utility and industrial customers. The paralysis was exacerbated by redundant mines awaiting closure, an alleged rail transportation monopoly, pricing problems in the former subsidized industry, and above all, a need for investment funds to replace obsolete mining equipment in the new competitive system. No doubt other interests could advance claims and assign blame, but the industry as a package certainly qualified for "restructuring," the term adapted from Gorbachev's prescription of *perestroika* for Russia's backward-looking economy.

In human terms, the aging, long-term miners could not easily relocate or retrain, having spent their lives in company-towns where employment included hospital and child-care, as well as housing and other communal benefits, still available. The union movement, only mildly aggressive by capitalist-country standards, its leaders enjoying rest-homes and other property inherited from the old regime, at least provided a voice for the miners' complaints, inevitably directed at the Yeltsin government. The call for a one-day national strike in March 1997 was inspired by coal-industry rage. Over 1.8 million Russians reportedly struck, but the movement quickly subsided, difficult to coordinate in a country with eleven time-zones and a populace tired of radical change. If a counter-revolution succeeds in reversing democratic capitalism in Russia, it is more likely to be accomplished at the ballot-box than at the barricades.

* * *

The World Bank made its first payment of $250 million on the $525 million coal-mine project in July 1995. The object was not only to shut down unprofitable mines and otherwise modernize the industry, but also to help fund a social safety-net for the soon-to-be-dismissed miners, a forecast of the new welfare concern that would distinguish the Bank's $6 billion 1997 program. The Russian government was also to contribute to the project, on the theory that co-payments involve greater responsibility for all concerned.

The World Bank made it clear it did not want its money to go into the coffers of Rosugol, the country's left-over giant Soviet-era coal monopoly, still state-owned and Russia's largest coal producer. In fact, its agreement for the loan specified plans for auctioning off the

Rosugol state shares to "trust" managers under a contract with the Russian government to operate the business. These trust managers, companies, banks or other qualified investors, would agree to privatize the shares to themselves or other investors at some vague point where the enhanced value would make the process feasible, the capitalist goal of good management and profitable growth fulfilled, and the government cashed out.

Rosugol's powerful Director, Yuri Malyshev, resisting this threat to his monopoly, pounced on a tactical error by the Bank. The Bank had agreed to make its loan directly to Russia's operating budget, relying on government agencies to redirect the money to local authorities in the impoverished mining areas. Months went by but the money never arrived. "We paid regular visits to those areas," the World Bank's Russia director said, "but no money arrived, so far as we know."[8] Prime Minister Chernomyrdin typically blamed a top Finance Ministry official for ignoring instructions. Finally, the harassed Bank held up the $275 million second portion of the loan, but eventually paid it out in November 1996. Malyshev remained on the offensive. The $250 million had failed to reach the coal mining regions or the producers, he said, and as far as he was concerned, Russia's coal industry could do without the World Bank loans, or state support either, he added, throwing a low blow for non-intervention by the state. "Rosugol wants to keep its monopoly," explained a high official in the coal-ministry.[9] Meanwhile, Anatoly Chubais, a tough, experienced economist-administrator, back in Yeltsin's cabinet as another first-deputy prime minister, entered the fray. He ordered a probe of the coal-miners' allegations that the entire $525 million was misspent by the mine-owners. "We were very pleased to hear of Mr. Chubais's decision to verify the use of funds channelled to the coal industry in recent months," states a World Bank information briefing. "The first loan appears to have reached the intended beneficiaries," it continues, "but so far there is no confirmation of the proper use of the second flow of funds." The terms of the loan for budget-use did not require auditing, it adds, and the Bank depended on the government's commitment to undertake coal-industry reforms, demonopolize the industry, and strengthen the safety-net for the miners and their communities.[10]

* * *

38

How could the World Bank fall into this contretemps when IMF had already learned the hard way, from early 1995 on, to disburse funds only by monthly payments, in order to maintain leverage? How could a *nomenklatura* like Malyshev, although apparently a seasoned executive with a thorough knowledge of his industry, defy both Yeltsin's cabinet and the World Bank? The episode will play itself out, and Russia will someday have efficient and privatized coal mines. It emphasizes the complexity and perhaps the inevitability of false starts in Russia's march to capitalism, with foreign aid increasingly important as the transition winds down.

My Problem with Gazprom's Taxes

Introduction

If a light moment is permitted on the subject of Russia's transition, now may be the time, when tragedy and farce still compete, but signs of success loom on the horizon. My favorite reporter on post-Cold War Russia is David Remnick, whose sure instinct for underlying truths is frequently laced with humor. His many cultural admirers, like Tatyana Tolstaya, say he writes very much in the darkly humorous spirit of Gogol.[11] If that is correct then Gogol too would have delighted in the extraordinary cast of vivid transition characters, Gorbachev, Yeltsin, Solzhenitsyn, Sakharov, even Zhirinovsky, the populist reincarnation of America's Huey Long. By the time Remnick visits others, the gang who couldn't shoot straight in the putsch against Gorbachev, the hack writers and artists lamenting their lost subsidies, the hopelessly indoctrinated and bereft older generation, the predatory millionaires shielded by dark glasses and bodyguards in Moscow's clean and corrupt elegance, the nation overwhelmed with grief at the gunning-down of Vladimir Listyev, the TV icon-magnate who connected so thoroughly with Russia's TV-dependent masses that he received a martyr's funeral comparable to Stalin's, we may as well be reading a canonical Russian novel.

The idea of a Russian novel recurs when reading the experiences of eminent palace advisors like Anders Åslund and Richard Layard, who open their books with a *dramatis personae* to help us keep track of the numerous deputy prime ministers, sometimes three at a time, central bankers, economists in orbit, rotating cabinet ministers, and deadly parliamentary opposition figures. The books end with a year-by-year chronology of notable political and economic events, a necessary guide for so much happening in so few years. Nor is humor absent, as they describe Yeltsin issuing duplicate, sometimes triplicate, decrees in the first heady days of radical reform, to offset subverted or lost originals in parliament, and hapless foreign-aid officials roaming the corridors, unable to place their elaborate proposals in the right hands.

The Problem

The following is based on phone conversations and faxes, in early 1997, between the author and high-level staff members in the Russian Division, World Bank, Washington, DC.

Author:	"Thank you for the information you faxed. I guess I am lucky to get to you."
World Bank:	"Well, we're all pretty busy, travelling to Russia frequently nowadays. So most requests like yours go to our Public Relations Department."
Author:	"I am particularly interested in Gazprom as a paradigm for understanding Russia's budget-deficit problems, from my view as a former financial executive as well as author. You didn't answer my question about the nature of Gazprom's tax payments."
World Bank:	"What difference does it make how the taxes were paid? I gather that is your question."
Author:	"It makes a lot of difference. Russia is desperate for cash to pay public employees, coal-miners, whatever. Tax reform dominates your own publications, for example, your current newsletter.[12] If taxes were being paid as expected, there might not have been the national one-day strike last week. It's one of Russia's worst

40

	problems, spoiling all the progress. And the rumors that taxes have been siphoned off to Chernomyrdin and Gazprom insiders don't encourage tax payments."
World Bank:	"You refer to the box on page 119 of *From Plan to Market*, World Development Report, 1996, box 7.1, 'Into the lion's den: Taxing Gazprom.' I checked with the author. That was the best information available at the time."
Author:	"Well, all I want is a breakdown. It says Gazprom paid taxes in 1995 of about $4 billion, and maybe owed twice as much to start with. That's a lot of money, considering World Bank's loans to Russia are only $6.4 billion since Yeltsin took over. How much was paid in cash, how much was cancelled by giving the government Gazprom stock or notes, how much by making a deal for accounting changes, like billions in reserves needed for capital equipment or pipelines? I think World Bank is entitled to that information. Even General Motors didn't pay federal income taxes of $4 billion in 1995."
World Bank:	"Gazprom is comparable to General Motors. $27 billion sales."
Author:	"You can do better than that. My question relates to the effectiveness of economic reform, regardless of Gazprom's power and value to the state. I remind you President Wolfensohn has assured me of all cooperation."
World Bank:	(Pause.) "I'll get back to you."

* * *

World Bank:	"We've done some checking and I was asked to call you. First of all, Gazprom paid $5.3 billion in taxes in 1995, not $4 billion."

41

Author:	"A 25% difference! The $4 billion figure has already gotten around. David Remnick refers to it in his new book, *Resurrection: The Struggle for a New Russia*.[13] Maybe he relied on the same World Bank Report. How was it paid?"
World Bank:	"Well, I have to tell you hard-information is not easy to get. Gazprom is very secretive. On anecdotal and unofficial evidence, I find you are right about a very substantial amount being paid via non-cash schemes. Here is our best knowledge: 1. $1.2 billion securitized by Gazprom notes. 2. 1.9 billion from excise taxes. 3. 1.1 billion from export taxes. 4. 1.1 billion possibly from corporate taxes on profit. <u>$5.3 billion total.</u>"
Author:	"As far as I can see, only No. 4 counts if Gazprom is now a 60%-privatized company trying to operate in the market system. Nos. 2 and 3 are simply skimmed off the top, no different from the way they were in the old days of the Soviet Union. So the reported payment of $4 billion 'from the lion's den' is ambiguous. It looks like only $1 billion paid from operating profits at best."
World Bank:	"Is there anything else?"
Author:	"No, I guess it's see your newspaper for further developments. First-Deputy Prime Minister Nemtsov seems to be making Gazprom a personal priority. He says if they paid the $2.6 billion taxes they still owe, it would take care of the back wages of all the state doctors, teachers, and kindergarten workers in the country. He has given them a deadline. If they haven't got the

cash, let them raise it in the world financial markets."[14]

* * *

G-7 Countries, European Commission, US Aid, and EBRD

The Group of Seven Countries was established in 1985, an organization of the leading industrial economies, United States, Japan, Germany, Britain, France, Canada, and Italy. It may soon be G-8, since Russia heads the waiting list. Russia qualifies as a friendly market-nation, though not as a leading industrial economy. Its present gross national product, after years of decline, is about $360 billion, placing it in the same group as Mexico, South Korea, and the Netherlands, but the assumption is Russia will be a leader in the twenty-first century, and there is a desire to offer it recognition.

Yeltsin has been invited to G-7 meetings, but as noted in chapter 1, he bears the memory of spectacular undelivered promises, when most needed, $25 billion of unspecified aid in April 1992, and $28 billion in April 1993. The G-7 organization is not an aid agency. It is frequently concerned with imposing economic sanctions against terrorist or similarly malevolent nations. In another role, its meetings, presided over by top finance ministers, will bargain over the strength of the yen, or lately the dollar, as they affect exports among member countries. Still the G-7 countries effectively control the IMF and the World Bank, as well as the European Commission (the economic arm of the 15-member European Union), so its significance for Russian aid is paramount. The inability of G-7 finance ministers to speak with political authority was noted in chapter 1. Richard Layard believes an active response by G-7 would have accelerated Russia's progress, and pain relief, by three years.[15] Since their aid overlaps, the two organizations can be combined as follows:

G-7 and European Commission Aid to Russia for 1992–1996

	$ billions
1. Outright grants (cash)	6
2. Loans (easy repayment terms but tied to buy exports from donor countries)	<u>18</u>
	24

(IMF Paper No. 133, December 1995, Table 7.11.
European Commission no longer processes Russian aid.)

From Russia's point of view, the loan credits, in many instances for surplus agricultural products from the US, were a mixed blessing, often aiding the donor countries as much as Russia itself.[16] The tied-credit loans can therefore be discounted by 25%.

Preliminary total aid: 1992–1996 and beyond

	$ billions
1. IMF (including future disbursements)	20.9
2. World Bank (including new projects)	12.4
3. G-7 and European Commission (adjusted)	<u>19.5</u>
	52.8

US Aid under the Freedom Support Act

Note should be taken of US aid to Russia under the Freedom Support Act, passed by Congress in 1992. The grants, varying widely from year to year, with only $95 million in 1996, total $2.1 billion through 1996. Much of this money has been used in conjunction with other agency objectives, such as pilot projects with the World Bank in the Russian privatization program.

This aid is separate from the better-known US SEED Act of 1989 (Seed Assistance to European Democracy), also administered by the Agency for International Development (AID) of the State Department. SEED does not include Russia. It has, however, distributed $2.7 billion to date to Central European countries, about half of that going to Poland, Hungary and Czechoslovakia. Many believe the earlier SEED legislation was an immediate response by Congress to

Americans of Central-European ancestry, celebrating the fall of the Berlin Wall. Russia was a slow-starter in gaining US sympathy. At any rate, $2.1 billion under the Freedom Support Act can be added to the provisional Russian total.[17]

EBRD (European Bank for Reconstruction and Development)

EBRD should not be confused with IBRD, although the acronyms are of little help. IBRD, as noted, is the World Bank lending agency, in the forefront, with IMF, of major new aid to Russia at the brink. EBRD, headquartered in London, commenced operations only in 1991, the year of Yeltsin's accession. Its sole reason for existence is to help the 26 countries of the former Soviet Union, from Armenia to Uzbekistan, make the transition to market economies. Russia is EBRD's largest client, although only one of many, and quite neglected in EBRD's early years.

As far as ideology is concerned, EBRD has no problem. It is unabashedly capitalist, so dedicated to privatization it has set a target of 60% to private beneficiaries compared with state-owned infrastructure. It wants its money used primarily to promote private and entrepreneurial initiative, and it abhors monopoly or other forms of centralization. EBRD is not concerned with social relief for transition victims, possibly on the assumption that relief will trickle down when the engine starts.

EBRD is the wild card of foreign aid. After considerable turmoil in 1993, EBRD was reorganized in 1994. By that time Russia had drawn down only $315 million in loans or other investments from EBRD. Now EBRD is the requisite center of attention for doing business in the former Communist countries. Its annual meeting in March 1997 was attended by 5,300 delegates, a worldwide assembly of industrialists, investment and central bankers, consultants, and intermediaries, a good omen for the eventual success of the transition to capitalism. At the meeting, EBRD announced its total assets had passed $13 billion, up from $10 billion in 1995. Other than IMF and the World Bank, it is the largest lender in Eastern Europe, without deposits or a central bank to augment its resources. It committed $2.4 billion in new money in 1995 and \$2.7 billion in 1996. EBRD at the end of 1996 had disbursed or made commitments for loans, investment funds, and equity positions in the amount of \$9 billion. Russia's share is \$1.6 billion of this amount.[18]

Some say EBRD is too commercial, more like a venture capital company or aggressive lender than an aid agency, citing its affinity for safe projects with blue-chip partners like Fiat, Coca Cola, and Samsung. Others question its profit motive for a non-taxpaying public agency; it posted \$6.1 million profit for 1996. On balance, EBRD has been not only a great success on its own terms, but it has also helped pave the way for Russia's ultimate transition strategy, foreign direct investment, such as Gazprom's initial public foreign offering, described in chapter 1. It can be added to Russia's foreign aid as follows:

Total Aid to Russia: 1992–1996 and beyond

		\$ billions
1. Preliminary total		52.8
2. US under Freedom Support Act		2.1
3. EBRD		<u>1.6</u>
	Total	56.5

The Paris and London Club Debts Owed by Russia

Placing a figure on total Western aid is an imprecise exercise at best, depending on variables such as the time-period covered, and whether or not to include funds committed but not yet disbursed, as the transition nears its end. Finally, there is the matter of what to exclude, for example, the downward adjustment of G-7 loans tied to exports from the donor countries, used in the above progression to a \$56.5 billion total.

The most important eligibility decision is how to treat the deferred Paris (countries) and London (banks) debts owed by Russia. The IMF, for example, includes debt deferment, granted and pending, in the amount of \$31.5 billion, in reaching a total of \$58.4 billion of foreign assistance to Russia in a 1995 analysis.[19]

In chapter 1, n.4, we listed Paris and London Club loans from the

Western countries alone at $42 billion, noting Germany's predominant $18 billion of this amount. Below are updated figures, including loans from Communist countries such as North Korea, Vietnam, and some former Soviet republics, obtained by Gorbachev and his predecessors:

Russia's Paris and London Club Debts 1991–1996[20]

	$ billions
Beginning of period	80.3
Deferred	59.6
Net amount owed by Russia	20.7

Should the $59.6 billion, or even the lesser amount of Western-country deferments of $42 billion, be considered foreign aid? They should not. Yeltsin only gestured to make good on these loans of the former Soviet Union when he took over in 1991, and he has now muddied the waters by asking to join the Paris Club, so Russia can collect *from* Communist countries, present and former, who in turn borrowed from the Soviet Union. Deferred debts are not foreign aid, as far as Russian citizens are concerned. When Russia recovers, the Paris and London Club obligations, for the most part, will enter the archives along with the bonds of the czars.

A Postscript on Germany

Germany, the largest and strongest economy in Europe, should be acknowledged for its generous aid as a G-7 country to Russia, but there is more to tell. Though far from Moscow, East Germany was as thoroughly converted to the Russian economic system as Hungary, Poland, and Czechoslovakia, and for the same time period. It is not treated as a transition country for the simple reason that West Germany, seeking reunification, took the entire burden of transition upon itself.

At the time of unification, East Germany, with a population of 19 million, a quarter of West Germany's, added a mere tenth to the combined gross national product. In one sense, economic transition was easier than in the former Soviet Union, since a market-framework of laws, institutions, and administrators was immediately available. Still, East Germany's low wages and productivity proved unfeasible in the unified country. The inevitable wage increases only aggravated East Germany's labor costs, resulting in massive unemployment. All in all, the transition costs are estimated at $700 billion in investments and social relief, unmatched in economic history, and a tribute to the capitalist capacity of the defeated nation. Germany's present high unemployment rate is related to the still laggard economy of the former German Democratic Republic. The report on Germany should also include its unique grant to Russia in 1993 to remove Russian occupation troops and provide housing funds on their return. At a cost of approximately $8 billion, Germany gave money a good name, cutting through the political negotiations with a practical, humanitarian solution.[21]

Evaluating Aid to Russia

Is approximately $55 billion, as above determined, enough from the West? How do you put a price on the end of antagonism between Western democracy and a powerful dictatorship, fortified by closed borders and secret police in Central and Eastern Europe for fifty years? What price can be put on the limitation of nuclear war, or on hopes for a new century of peace and prosperity?

Neither democracy nor the market-economy can be purchased by foreign aid, no matter how much is expended, or how it is categorized. If Russia reaches both destinations, it will be through the pain and fortitude of the Russians themselves, drawing on their great natural resources, immense national pride, and tremendous human talent. Finally, it will be because the Russian people will intellectually decide it is unreasonable to return to their former system, regardless of economic security, compared with the competing environment of political freedom and its dynamic ally, economic freedom. This decision will be not only a matter of rational choice, but also one emotionally-conditioned by TV, where both democracy and the market-system are subject to relentless examination, and still surpass the alternative. Of course, there is a cautionary note for transition countries: new political freedom can stand imperfections, but new economic freedom, unless it benefits a distinct majority of voters in a reasonable time-frame, will become unacceptable. There will be too many losers.

* * *

Having said this, the fact remains that foreign aid from the West probably tipped the balance in favor of Russia's success. $50 to $60 billion is a respectable amount, and no one should ask who lost Russia for want of more. Some summary conclusions follow:

1 The aid was too little and too late in the first three years. Russia barely survived this period without reverting to the old order and its powerful constituency, the military-industrial-populist complex, laying in wait.

2 Diversion of aid to social relief came only when Russia was at the brink.

3 Economic reform was treated as a traditional financial problem rather than related to a political revolution. More political concern would have anticipated the effects of the initial shock treatment.

4 IMF and World Bank inherited by default decisions and strategies that might better have come from a G-7 cabinet of the highest rank, led by a world-figure, perhaps a Jimmy Carter or Václav Havel. It is one of the anomalies of the transition that IMF and World Bank were able to move into the vacuum, and bypass legislatures and parliaments with billions of aid. They were never designed or intended for a transition role, but fortunately were available with staffs and resources in place.

5 Ideology entered the decision-process, reflecting the confident laissez-faire stance of the America-dominated IMF and World Bank. More European direction, at ease with necessary

government regulation, would have diminished Russia's economic gap.

6 Yeltsin's remarkable survival as a legitimate ruler from 1991 on gave strength and continuity to the transition process, resulting in increasing levels of aid. Though frequently backsliding, as a weak president must, and tarnished by Chechnya, Yeltsin stayed the course for both radical reform and democracy.

7 Comparisons of Russian aid and the Marshall Plan, although inevitable, are not relevant. The total Marshall Plan expenditure, all from America, has finally sifted down by consensus, on the Plan's fiftieth anniversary. It was $7 billion then, worth $115 billion now.[22]

Approximately half was in the form of goods and services, not cash. Europe was physically destroyed and many countries faced starvation, justifying this approach. Historians tell us that Marshall Plan officials campaigned effectively to gain the consent of the recipient countries, since 50% counterpart funds were expected from those able to pay. It was still a grand bargain, but Russia decided to have none of it.

Another major difference: the Marshall Plan was a matter of outright grants to prostrate countries and not of repayable loans. Russia in 1991 was an advanced industrial country, brought down largely by Gorbachev's political reform, a dissolving empire, and a defense budget twice that of America as a per cent of gross domestic product. Over two-thirds of the aid from IMF, World Bank, G-7, and EBRD is secured by notes, which theoretically must be paid, forgetting the Paris and London Club creditors. Some of this debt has already been paid, such as IMF principal of $500,000 and interest to date described in chapter 1. Additionally, Russia has paid in approximately $5 billion to join the above three lending institutions, of which $1.25 billion was required to be paid in hard currencies, not rubles.[23] Eventually the interest alone on this debt burden will prove to be too high as a per cent of Russia's budget (the American problem), and adjustments will undoubtedly be made. There are essential differences between the Marshall Plan for Europe and Western aid for post-Communist Russia.

Notes

1 *World Bank Annual Report*, 1996, 173. Of World Bank's total capitalization of $180 billion, only $10.9 billion has been paid-in. The remaining $169 billion is "subject to call," but since most of it would be from G-7 countries, the Bank is able to borrow funds as needed on the basis of $180 billion net worth.

2 The party is ending for China and the World Bank. From now on, China will no longer receive subsidized, low-rate loans, according to Joseph Stiglitz, chief World Bank economist, and its $2 to $3 billion yearly allocation is under review. China can laugh its way to the impending exit from the Bank. In 1996 it received $52 billion, or 20%, of the record $285 billion of capital poured into the developing and transition countries. Russia received $3.6 billion. *Wall Street Journal*, 24 March 1997, 9A.

3 Paul Blustein, "Loan Ranger: James D. Wolfensohn and the World Bank," *The Washington Post*, 10 November 1996, 24–6.

4 *World Bank: Russia Economic Backgrounder*, 17 March 1997, 3.

5 "Gini-coefficients are a standard measure of equality of income distribution, calculated with reference to the departure of an actual distribution from a state of perfect income equality." "Definitions and Data Notes," *World Bank Development Report 1996* (New York: Oxford University Press, 1996), viii.

6 World Bank, *Transition*, February 1997, 3.

7 The case for consolidation of functions is illustrated by variations in important statistics between the two agencies. There is perhaps no figure more important than the annual change in Russia's budget deficits as a per cent of gross domestic product (see chapter 1, n.3). World Bank produced a figure for 1995 substantially higher than IMF's. Both agencies are committed to reducing Russia's inflationary deficits as a top priority, and IMF threatens to withhold monthly payments if deficit-reduction goals are not met. How could such a vital measure of Russia's progress vary

51

substantially in a recent year? Answer: one agency adds back to GDP a significant amount for the unreported or black-market economy, the other uses a different "deflator" for previous years' inflation, and both employ different time-series for GDP.

The Economist, analyzing the World Bank, deplores its failure rate and duplication. It gives credit to President Wolfensohn's restructuring plan, but observes, "the 180 governments which own it would not bother to create it now." (1 March 1997, 22).

8 *The RUSSIAN*, March 1997, 19.

9 *Ibid.*, 21.

10 From the Director of World Bank's Moscow office, provided by David Craig, coal-project task-manager, 8 April 1997.

11 Tatyana Tolstaya, "The Way They Live Now," *The New York Review of Books*, 24 April 1997, 13.

12 Deputy US Treasury Secretary Lawrence Summers, speaking to a conference of US and Russian businessmen at Kennedy School of Government, Harvard University, quoted in World Bank, *Transition*, February 1997, 5: "Two things in particular keep [foreign investment] capital at arm's length: the tax system and corruption."

13 David Remnick, *Resurrection, the Struggle for a New Russia* (New York: Random House, 1997), 178.

14 Gazprom will probably raise the cash. It recently announced a line of credit from a group of international banks for $4.2 billion for pipeline construction, not guaranteed by the government. *Transition*, January 1997, 26; *Wall Street Journal*, 17 June 1997, A3.

15 Layard, *The Coming Russian Boom*, 298.

16 See Åslund, *How Russia Became a Market Economy*, 164, 218. Western countries offered Russia $12.5 billion in commodity credits in 1992. The exports were purchased at subsidized prices, contributing to Russia's inflation. This undermined Russian financial stabilization and did so for the benefit of Western farm lobbies, Åslund states. Jeffrey Sachs has also made this charge, castigating IMF for promoting the program. Boris Federov finally sharply reduced the commodity credits in early 1993.

17 To put a better face on US aid to Russia and the other former Soviet countries:

US Aid Through 1996 ($ billions)

Freedom Support Act to Russia	2.1
Freedom Support Act to eleven newly independent states, surrounding Russia,from Armenia to Uzbekistan	2.8
SEED Act to Central European countries (excluding Russia)	2.7
US contribution to G-24/European Commission (now excluding Russia), 7.5 cash, 5.5 mostly exports (through 1995)	<u>13.0</u>
	20.6

Source: Freedom Support Act and SEED reports, 1996. Presentations to Congress, FY 1998, US Agency for International Development, State Department

Add to this $450 million direct to Ukraine for the destruction of strategic nuclear missiles, and an estimated $700 million since 1989 from citizen-at-large George Soros for transforming Soviet-bloc countries into capitalist democracies, and the total is in the $22 billion range.

18 EBRD, *Annual Report*, 1996, 64. The shares of EBRD are owned by 60 member countries. EBRD has only $4 billion paid-in capital, of which $3.2 billion is from G-7 countries. Like World Bank, it has pledges of $3.3 billion it can call on, mostly from G-7 countries, and can accordingly borrow funds as needed. (EBRD, *Annual Report*, 1996, 67)

19 Eduard Brau, "External Financial Assistance: The Record and Issues," Occasional Paper 133, *Policy Experiences and Issues in the Baltics, Russia, and Other Countries of the Former Soviet Union*, IMF, December 1995, Table 7.5, 111.

20 Letter from Daniel Citrin, Chief, Russian Division, International Monetary Fund, dated 30 April, 1997.

21 In addition to its East Germany expenditures, Germany has contributed over $20 billion through G-7/European Commission for aid to Russia and

the Central European countries. The Russian troops removal was negotiated by Gorbachev in 1991, only a few months before his ouster. Gorbachev settled for $8 billion cash and $2 billion more in interest-free credits, for removal and housing in Russia within four years. (See Tony Judt, "New Germany, Old NATO," *New York Review of Books*, 29 May 1997, 38.) The German Consulate, Los Angeles, has provided the author with information (13 May 1997) that a total of $11 billion was paid for troops removal, of which $3 billion was for social benefits for the unemployed troops. Germany's major contributions to the success of transition must be acknowledged.

22 For an excellent, comprehensive up-date of the Marshall Plan, by participants, historians, and experts, see "The Marshall Plan and Its Legacy," a commemorative section in *Foreign Affairs*, May/June 1997, edited by Peter Grose, 159–220.

23   Amounts paid by Russia to join aid agencies (billions)

	Due on joining agency	Payable in hard currency, (dollars, yen, etc.)	
IMF	4,500	1,120	(25%)
World Bank	334	33	(10%)
EBRD	213	106	(50%)
	5,047	1,259	

World Bank and EBRD entry fees are nominal, subject to calls for much larger subscriptions, not likely to be exercised or paid.

4 Russia, Hungary, Poland, and the Czech Republic Compared

The Economic Strategies of Transition

A comparison can be made between on-the-brink Russia and the three Central European success stories of economic transition, Hungary, Poland, and the Czech Republic, but no ready conclusions can be drawn about the differing results from similar strategies.

The transition strategy for each country appears to be uniform. After gaining unexpected "velvet-glove" political freedom, the next step, in a rush of enthusiasm for radical reform, was to terminate the totalitarian economic system, tainted by its former political alliance, and rapidly disintegrating as well. The economy was no longer protected by isolation from the outside world. It was no longer organized by the threat of war and mind-numbing propaganda.

The strategy at the outset called for a sudden ending of price controls and foreign trade restrictions, and the introduction of convertible currency. This was a signal to home and abroad that the market-system would prevail. Commonplace phrases like "the window of opportunity" were invoked by harassed planners for unplanning, aware that their political leadership depended on the shaky coalitions of democracy, and that vested bureaucratic interests throughout the economic system would be in sharp opposition.

Following this bold deregulation, the next strategy was to set in motion the privatization of enterprises, which in all four countries consisted of nearly-100% state ownership or control, including the professions and media. As a related privatization strategy, the transition of state-owned residences and farms to private-property status was put on the drawing board. These formidable tasks alone were unprecedented for a democratic state. It is to Yeltsin's great credit that he managed to preside over the biggest unscrambling of all for almost a decade.

Finally, guided by Western aid agencies, and by a new breed of transition-economists, domestic and foreign, each country embraced the doctrine of painful restraints on government subsidies and cradle-to-grave social services, and subscribed to a new concept of budget-deficit reduction based on Western accounting. These financial goals, the least understood of the complex strategy, were regarded as essential for becoming a market economy. They were also deemed necessary for holding in line the severe inflation expected from the instant ending of price controls.

Transition-strategy was not a response to a depression crisis, well-known and feared in the Western world. For years Soviet-occupied countries emphasized production and military might rather than consumption goods, many of which were subsidized or frowned upon to start with. As a result of relatively full employment at low wages, there was a tremendous overhang of purchasing power in each country available for every kind of consumer item, bound to push up prices for whatever dribbled onto the static market, a market reluctant to learn classic textbook laws of supply and demand. Money was not yet hidden under mattresses or sent abroad, as it would be when real wages and gross domestic product eventually crashed, exacerbating the damage already caused by excessive inflation. In retrospect, observers can ask why the overhanging money was not frozen, or called into the banking system in exchange for time-deposits or government savings-notes, an action in scope similar to Roosevelt's freezing of gold and its convertibility in 1933. One answer may lie in the dominance of market theory as a new theology, with little patience for pragmatic government action.

Out of this maelstrom, "shock therapy" was added to the lexicon of economic terminology. Each of the four countries experienced different degrees of shock therapy, depending on which group and how many of its citizens happened to stand in the line of fire. Shock therapy was a by-product, if not an intent of radical reform. It should be kept in mind when examining the following comparative tables.

* * *

56

Overall view (excluding privatization, treated ahead)

	Year radical reform starts and head of state	Population 1996 (millions)	Gross domestic product ($ billions) 1996
Russia	1991 (Boris Yeltsin)	148.4*	392
Hungary	1989–90 (Joszef Antall)	10.2	39
Poland	1990 (Lech Walesa)	38.3	95
Czechoslovakia	1989 (Václav Havel)	10.3	33

*3.5 mill. decline

(Economist)

* * *

Major pain factors

Annual per cent increase (decrease) in rate of inflation

	1990	1991	1992	1993	1994	1995	1996	Average 1989–1995
Russia	5.6	92.7	1,353.0	896.0	303.0	190.0	47.8	222.1
Hungary	29.0	34.2	22.9	22.5	19.0	28.2	23.6	24.5
Poland	586.0	70.3	43.0	35.3	32.2	27.8	19.9	101.6
Czech Republic	10.8	56.7	11.1	20.8	10.2	9.1	9.0	20.4

Annual per cent increase (decrease) in gross domestic product

	1990	1991	1992	1993	1994	1995	1996	Average 1990–1994
Russia	-3.6	-5.0	-14.5	-8.7	-12.6	-4.0	-5.0	-14.8
Hungary	-2.5	-7.7	-4.3	-2.3	2.5	2.0	1.0	-1.0
Poland	-11.6	-7.0	2.6	3.8	5.5	7.0	5.5	0.3
Czech Republic	-1.2	-14.2	-6.4	-0.5	2.6	5.0	4.2	-4.9

(1990–1995: World Bank, *From Plan to Market*, 1995. 1996: IMF, *World Economic Outlook*, May, 1997. Average: Economist)

* * *

58

Quality of life

	Per cent of population in poverty (1996)	Life expectancy (men) (1996)	Per cent of unemployment and underemployment (1996)
Russia	25	62	9.3
Hungary	15–20	65	10.5
Poland	15–20	67	13.0
Czech Republic	5–10	68	3.0
	(World Bank) (Estimates)	(Economist)	(World Bank; US SEED Report 1997)

Foreign aid from the West (disregarding Paris and London Club debt deferment) 1991–1996 ($ billions disbursed)

	From international agencies (World Bank, IMF, EBRD)	From US Freedom Support Act and SEED	From G-24/European Commission	Total
Russia	22.0	2.100	24.0	48.1
Hungary	6.0	.228	10.6	16.8
Poland	7.0	.848	8.0	15.8
Czech Republic	1.0	.147	3.3	4.4

(G-24 no longer processes aid to Russia. Above $24 billion for Russia is from G-7 countries prior to this change. EBRD and G-24 include amounts committed. G-24 figures from Brussels headquarters, as of 1 November 1996, for 1990–1995.)

* * *

Other transition objectives

Private foreign investment
1991–1996 ($ billions)
Source: EBRD

Russia	5.1
Hungary	13.2
Poland	4.9
Czech Republic	6.6

Budget deficit (-) or surplus as per cent of gross
domestic product.IMF generally requires
maintaining 4% or less deficit.

	1994	1995
Russia	-10.50	-4.26
Hungary	-6.10	-3.70
Poland	-2.32	.02
Czech Republic	.90	.05

Sources of budget deficits: IMF *World Outlook*, October 1996. Budget deficit figures vary widely among agencies and are frequently adjusted, but the trends are acceptable. Russia's 1996 deficit is estimated at -7.0 per cent and 1997's first quarter shows little change.

* * *

Reviewing the above figures, it is likely that one would choose to live last in Russia during the past decade. Especially if you were on a pension, a collective farm, or connected with the elaborate state machinery of bureaucrats, engineers, teachers, soldiers, athletes, economists (more per thousand than in market societies), and other *apparatchiks* and functionaries of a top-heavy, disintegrating welfare state. The real killer was the inflation rate, bounding along from each year's prior base, until by 1993 it had wiped out the ruble's pre-reform value. Gone were not just the life-savings, less important in a welfare-society, but the comparative security traded-off for personal freedom by three generations of Russians, most of whom believed in the system, lacking any stronger belief. They were galvanized in that direction by World War II and the Cold War.

The experience would be less traumatic if it were primarily a matter of reporting to work for a new market-system boss, but as the figures show, Russia's gross domestic product has melted away compared with the three success-countries. The latter have recovered their GDP starting points. Their political and economic achievements have been rewarded with imminent NATO membership. They are candidates for membership in the European Union, with its great free-trade benefits, assuming they can maintain 3% or less budget-deficits as a percent of GDP. In recent years they were admitted to the 29-member OECD (Organization for Economic Cooperation and Development), another step in appeasing their century-old self-perception as peripheral states, excluded from partnership in European trade and politics.[1]

Russia, by contrast, is a far-flung, immense country of diverse ethnic groups. It is burdened with the clogged arteries of industrial dinosaurs, and no longer trades as the dominant power in a closed world of its own. It had little prior understanding of capitalism and its rules. In short, it has been unable to make even a seven-year transition without excessive pain and a last-minute bailout by the international aid agencies. By most accounts, Russia still operates at a gross domestic product only two-thirds of its starting point. GDP is the icon of capitalism. It generates the jobs and taxes that pay for consumer satisfaction, and for the increments of social protection adopted by capitalism during its two centuries of trial and error. GDP cannot be overlooked.

* * *

Additionally the overall figures remind us of Russia's misery-index, a fourth of the population in the poverty class, at a time when social relief in the transition countries is associated with excessive subsidies, rightly regarded as dysfunctional if the immediate goal is an efficient market system. Only the unemployment figure seems tolerable, on the surface less than that of Germany, the powerhouse of European capitalism and generous contributor to the transition countries. The figure is disguised by hang-in, low-wage employees, unable to budge from their shell-shocked, cash-strapped employers, who resist the call to downsize, and by a large percentage of underground or black-market workers.

This is not to gainsay the vitality of the Russian economy, finally on the brink of positive yearly growth in GDP, selling off its crown jewels of natural gas and oil for billions of non-inflationary cash, its inflation just about ended, and its cities booming with construction. Russia is attracting a new wave of loans and investments from the outside world. Foreign aid, as noted, is arriving at record levels, a good deal reserved for social relief. In the long run, wars, plagues, famine, and natural disasters are more serious than economic cycles. The transition costs for Russia have been great, certainly far more than necessary, but as Adam Smith, the father of capitalist theory, observed about the capacity to recover, there is a lot of ruin in nations.

* * *

If the misery-index of poverty, unemployment, and inflation for Hungary, Poland, and the Czech Republic in the above tables indicates success, then a large percentage of citizens would decline the honor. The success is substantial, but only relative compared with Russia's long-haul and the bleak prospects of the other Central and East European countries in transition, with the exception of the Baltic countries.

One misery-index category, poverty, should be examined at the risk of showing inadequate feeling. The poverty group in America is over 30 million, representing an intractable 12 to 14 per cent of the population for decades, with children in the 20% area. Most of the defined poor (for example, a family of four with less than $14,500 income), are single-mothers with dependent children, on welfare. If social security and medical benefits had not been provided for America's rapidly-aging senior population, the poverty figure would possibly be double, regardless of prosperity. Without question, to be poor in a transition country, especially Russia, must be far more shattering than in an advanced industrial society. There the poor cope by moving in with their families, scrounging for work, and foregoing basic food, health, and recreation. Still the poverty figure alone should not disqualify the comparative success of Hungary, Poland, and the Czech Republic. The trends are favorable for at least three years and should be celebrated. Growth in employment, hopefully at increasing wages related to productivity, and increasing GDP, are the key factors.

Reflections on the "Success-Trio"

Transition experience varies considerably from country to country, depending greatly on political factors and pre-reform conditions, as well as on the official ideology. Some highlights for each of the "success-trio" will expand our knowledge and remind us that Russia was only one of the players in the historic political and economic transformation at the end of the twentieth century.

Note that the trio, their velvet-revolutions accomplished in the same time-frame as the symbolic fall of the Berlin Wall in 1989, have received to date about $36 billion of foreign aid, compared with Russia's approximate $50 billion. Money is a weak measure when freedom, even economic freedom, is at stake. Still, if we want an accounting, as capitalism requires, of where so many billions were spent after the Cold War terminated, six years after the money began to flow is timely, especially when one can evaluate whether the aid was adequate and effective.

Russia *in extremis* has another dozen billions in the pipeline from IMF, World Bank, and EBRD, but the success-trio understandably have reached the bottom of the well, and soon will be on their own. Hungary surprisingly has received as much as Poland, a country with three times Hungary's population and GDP. The Czech Republic is low-man on the receiving line, unwilling to accept the agency-control and debt-burden accompanying the international largesse. Its very able Václav Klaus, a finance minister turned prime minister, and head of state for as long a period as Yeltsin in Russia, had his central bank repay IMF in full in the early years. The Czech Republic received its $800 million quota-refund, then rejoined later for modest borrowings of $250 million, compared with Hungary's $2.2 billion presently owed to IMF. Klaus, the only one of the trio's current leaders without a background of prior Communist affiliation, is fortified by an unwavering belief in free-market ideology. The less state intervention and subsidies, the better he likes it, although he pragmatically has used the state to hold down inflationary wage-increases, a strategy to which he attributes much of his success.[2] The Czech Republic's turnabout is now tarnished by serious fraud conditions in its banking, Stock Exchange, and privatization programs, indicating more regulation in the future, and threatening the Klaus regime.

Hungary: Gradualism and Foreign Investment Attraction

Although saddled with one of the highest foreign-debt ratios in Europe, and accordingly with a crushing debt-payment burden, much to the dismay of the foreign-aid monitors who supplied a good deal of the debt, Hungary has won distinction on two transition fronts.

First, it is distinguished by its gradualism. Not the gradualism of China's long march to capitalism, to be discussed in a later chapter, but the short-term gradualism of minimal shock-treatment after-effects arising from the strategy of overnight price and currency deregulation. Both Russia and Poland suffered immediate, long-term hyperinflation, as the inflation table shows, but Hungary's fever-chart stays steady over a seven-year period, approximately 20% increase per year. Part of this success arises from a background of market-freedom achieved during the Communist period, under the unpredictable but often accommodating 30-year regime of János Kádár. Some call this limited but aggressive reform "goulash Communism." At any rate it was an ingenious Hungarian brand of market-socialism, that over the years allowed most consumer prices to approach that of the trading world outside the Soviet orbit. Similar inroads were made in

64

the privatization of the retail and agricultural sectors and the decentralizing of manufacturing decisions, along with market-system taxation and commercial codes, pushed by a generation of intrepid reformers and dissenters. They were cruelly chastened by 4,000 Russian tanks in response to the 1956 uprising led by Imre Nagy and ignored by the Western world, but the cumulative effect eased the 1990's transition to capitalism.

Additionally, Hungary's misery index has been cushioned by deliberate resistance to wholesale reductions in social benefits, still draining a large part of the government budget. Hungary's relatively mild shock-experience helped it become the admired tortoise among the success-trio nations. Its record of financial institution regulation and corporate fraud-control in the post-Communist period is now offered as an example to the embarrassed Czech Republic, the previous front-runner. In 1996, the three major American credit-rating institutions upgraded Hungary and Poland to an investment-grade rating, meaning their bonds are eligible for Western universities, pension funds, and charitable foundations, and at lower interest rates to boot. There are those who understandably do not have such a rosy view of Hungary's accomplishments. After enduring the fascist regime of Admiral Horthy, and the oppressive regime of the Communists and their puppets, they had higher hopes for the new, democratic country.[3]

* * *

Hungary's second distinction lies in its ability to attract foreign investment, not only in foreign loans, such as Russia's critically helpful Eurobonds, but in foreign business investments, likely to create employment, gross domestic product, and the exports that define a robust, market-system nation.[4] Its approximate $14 billion in that area, from 1991 through 1996, is close to three times that of either Russia, Poland, or the Czech Republic. This edge reflects the relatively open, market-oriented economy achieved in the pre-democracy period, as noted. In the past decade, Hungary has developed a market-style legal and regulatory structure, complete with international accounting standards and bankruptcy and liquidation procedures, all reassuring to foreign firms seeking new entry or joint-venture for a share of the former Soviet markets, lured in the first place by low labor-costs accepted by grateful employees. In 1994, Hungary voted back into power the former Socialist Party, obviously dissatisfied with the new division of spoils, but the Party, already indoctrinated with doubt about the future of a command economy, realistically continues the march to capitalism and integration with Western Europe.

Another vital factor has attracted the billions in foreign investment, among the highest in the world in relation to population. Hungary's 1989 privatization program, the earliest among the success-trio, and three years ahead of Russia's xenophobic program, permitted the direct sale to foreigners of medium and large-size state enterprises. This heretical strategy discounted the traditional fear of foreign invasion through money, not arms. Even advanced countries, in their present binge of privatization, draw the line where national security, or even pride, may be involved. At any rate, Hungary, not an arms merchant to start with, offered open-house to new entrants and joint-ventures. First, industrial companies and mass retailers made their appearance. Later, infrastructure, energy, telecommunications, and banking went on the block. By 1996, according to the Hungarian Privatization Research Institute, more than two-thirds of the country's largest companies had significant foreign ownership, and foreign owners had majority shares in the utilities and banking sectors.[5] These enterprises form an important labor and output core of the economy, and account for more than half of the country's exports. Ironically, this sellout to the West was probably justified, at least for Hungary. As we will note in the next chapter on privatization, the initial distributions of state enterprises in Russia, Poland, and the Czech Republic were confined first to employees, followed quickly to the public at large, practically cost-free, presumably to make everyone an instant capitalist, but leaving enterprises short of working capital and independent management. This procedure, although politically correct, and perhaps the only choice, can backfire through insider-deals and lack of effective management control. The Hungarian land-scape, dotted with GE, General Motors, Pepsico, Ameritech, Ford, IBM, Wal-Mart, and similar names for European and Asian entries, along with less-visible foreign-venture ownership, is one where constant performance and dynamic change will be demanded, including forced bankruptcy and liquidation when necessary, with so many large investments on the line.

Poland: A Formidable Economist

Leszek Balcerowicz, an eminent, sober economics professor for twenty years, was unexpectedly tapped to become Poland's deputy prime minister and minister of finance in September 1989. In retrospect, no more qualified or self-confident economist could have been found to serve as architect of Poland's "shock therapy" transition. It was the year of Poland's first free election since becoming a Soviet satellite in the wake of the Potsdam Conference of 1945. Lech Walesa, a charismatic shipyard worker in Gdansk, on the Baltic coast, had worn down the chief of state, General Jaruzelski, unable to resist the Solidarity leader's demand for a place on the ballot, backed by a series of national strikes. Moreover, the general was doubtful Mikhail Gorbachev, a candidate for the 1990 Nobel Peace Prize Award, had the stomach to march in and save him. Walesa was allowed to run as a trade-union leader, although unions were illegal, to evade the regime's only-one-party rule, and surprisingly won the election. The new prime minister, Tadeusz Mazowiecki, was one of four prime ministers Balcerowicz would serve under until he resigned three years later, mission accomplished, in December 1992, a few month's after Gorbachev's ouster. When Balcerowicz left office, he wrote, he felt relief but not much more: "I am not a sentimental man."[6]

* * *

Where would such a detached and knowledgeable economist come from, in such a hectic period? He was not a Walesa functionary, although economic dissatisfaction was a primary focus of Solidarity's rage, fuelled by patriotic and religious contempt for the puppet regime. In fact, Solidarity's economics were part of the problem. Their demands for wage increases and lower prices, partially granted by the fumbling state, its economy distorted by demands for Soviet preferences, only added to the hyperinflation sweeping the country before Walesa took office. It was Balcerowicz's duty to convince

Walesa that government wage controls were necessary, although price controls must go, a particularly difficult task, he notes, for an administration uniquely in debt to a trade-union for its legitimacy. Walesa was a quick learner. Only a month after January 1990, when the radical reforms were announced, he made a critical endorsement on national radio: it was necessary to lower costs as well as prices by "fifty or even a hundred per cent."[7]

An additional duty Balcerowicz faced up to was the staggering inheritance of foreign debt from the socialist era, from nations represented by the Paris Club, and banks by the London Club. It is difficult to believe that several hundred leading Western banks steadily doled billions to Communist countries during the Cold War '70s and '80s, indirectly benefitting the Soviet war machine. Paris and London Club loans to Poland totalled $40 billion in 1990. The rationale for the banks must have been to extend an open window to the Soviet Union and its satellites, at profitable interest rates, since they had never defaulted. The country loans to Poland, the major part of the $40 billion, were two-thirds for credits to buy exports from the lending countries, equally suspect. Faced with galloping inflation, and an unqualified conviction that the economic system must be quickly reformed without distractions, Balcerowicz righteously negotiated for reduction rather than abrogation, although the debt payments were impossible to meet. After travelling constantly to the G-7 countries to beg for relief, including a non-committal meeting with President Bush, involved with America's own financial problems, and a side visit to Pope John Paul II for moral support, Balcerowicz finally saw some hope. President Walesa sent urgent letters to the G-7 countries, in advance of his impending trip to America for a hero's welcome. David Mulford, US Deputy Treasurer Secretary and Western spokesman for such debts, advised Balcerowicz that his request for 80% reduction was out of the question. "I may try to persuade them for 50%, but I will not fight for more." That was all Balcerowicz wanted in the first place, and the deal was made: Paris Club debts cancelled 30% now and 20% later, providing the pending IMF agreement, imposing strict budgetary restraints, was successfully completed.[8] London Club arrangements followed in due course.

* * *

What manner of man stood ready to take on the G-7 creditors, the international aid agencies, the vested *nomenklatura*, and Solidarity itself, as Poland became the first breakaway satellite nation, with only Hungary's gradualist model for nearby reference? This brings us into the special world of transition economists, briefly empowered with emergency legislative authority to invoke risky, jolting decrees on how entire nations should go about their getting and spending, without armies to back them up. All this in order to join the outside world of profit-driven trade and efficiency, portrayed to them as a valueless wasteland during most of their early education. The post-1989 years were a period when economists, called upon for their special knowledge of the psychological aspects of demand, the turning-on of dormant supply, of shock therapy to end hyperinflation, and of the mass privatization of enterprise, were agents of immense power. Faced with the decision to fight inflation with more inflation, and to cause great reductions in gross domestic product and social protection for an indeterminate period, rightly or wrongly, the transition economists did not retreat. Richard Layard notes that of Russia's five leading economist-reformers (Gaidar, Federov, Shokhin, Chubais, and Yavlinsky), each except Chubais formed his own political party,[9] and Chubais is presently a high-ranking politician for Yeltsin. It may be that in the West's global, peaceful phase, the time of the economist has come.

* * *

There was no Iron Curtain separating Balcerowicz from the Western world, although academics and professionals in the satellite countries had little choice but to come to terms with the system in order to survive and move ahead in their careers. After graduating from the Warsaw School of Economics, which apparently had the most Western-oriented faculty in the satellite countries, he spent 1972–1974 at St. John's University in New York. He then returned to Warsaw to teach international economics and obtain his PhD at Warsaw's Central School of Planning and Statistics, with side excursions to the University of Sussex in 1985 to study the South Korean "economic miracle," and to West Germany in 1988. By this time, Balcerowicz was a firm adherent of institutional economics, by his definition meaning that one system will perform better than another because of its institutional arrangements, for example, state ownership or private ownership of property, and not because of allegiance to utopian principles, or possession of great natural resources. This led to considerations of how to reform, given the possibility, an obviously inferior system.

By 1978 Balcerowicz had gathered an informal group of young economists working on an agenda for reform, meeting every week for two years, ostensibly within the system. When Solidarity erupted in 1980, the group recognized the startling possibilities of actual reform. Set back by martial law in 1981, imposed to discourage dissent, Balcerowicz resolutely resigned from Party membership, but the group emerged again in 1982. The pattern was similar to that surrounding Yegor Gaidar and his circle in Russia in the same period, and to a Václav Klaus earlier group in Czechoslovakia. Testing the limits in authoritarian countries, which were unable to suppress the flow of information in the new world of communications, must have given a heightened sense of mission to the economists, comparable to that of the political and intellectual dissenters, with their irrepressible underground journals.

Understandably, the economists, regarding the state and its political prisons as the enemy, chose the free-market system, already heralded for its accomplishments in the West, as the designated goal for radical change. Note also that not only Russia, but the trio of success-countries, had sophisticated, highly-able economists on hand to lead the transition, including, Hungary's Peter Bod, minister of finance, 1990–1991, and later head of the central bank.[10] They chose overnight deregulation of prices, budgetary austerity, currency convertibility, open foreign-trade, subsidy-reduction, mass-privatization, and varying degrees of shock therapy on the basis of their own rigorous analysis and observations. The role of the aid-agency officials and of the high-profile advisors from the Western nations on matters of strategy was of great value, but not indispensable.

The Pope and Capitalism

No story of the transition to capitalism is complete without acknowledging the role of John Paul II. Rarely has a religious figure exercised such political and moral influence on the world at large, preaching tirelessly to the multitudes which only he can summon. Born Karol Wojytla in Poland, and Pope since 1978, his overwhelming effect on his country's consciousness was fundamental to its becoming the first of the velvet-revolution sites, in 1989, after the Pope made common cause with the Solidarity labor movement. A born diplomat, statesman, and linguist, he seemed always to be in the right place at the right time, patiently admonishing the Soviets on behalf of his imprisoned cardinals, and dissidents of all faiths, carefully leaving the door open for the prodigal's return. Stalin's observation to the contrary, this Pope's moral authority has been worth countless divisions.

Less known is that John Paul II is not especially in harmony with the new, triumphant capitalism. He represents a cautionary influence in that respect. Leszek Balcerowicz tells how he calculatingly visited the Pope in 1990 for support in his campaign to the G-7 leaders to show mercy on his country's crushing Paris Club debts. The Pope received the economist cordially, but spent most of the 40-minute audience asking Balcerowicz how economic justice would be treated in the new economic order.[11]

It is not surprising that in May 1991, John Paul II issued a major encyclical "Centisimus Annus," on the economic questions raised in Eastern Europe. He warned the new capitalist nations that they must not let the collapse of Communism blind them to the need to repair inequities at home. The free market, the encyclical declared, while the most efficient instrument for utilizing resources, does not meet the human needs which find no place in the market. Capitalism must be circumscribed by a framework of laws and rights, it continued, as well as an ethical and religious understanding of human freedom.[12]

Poland's Shock Therapy

How does Balcerowicz justify shock therapy? The table indicates that the Walesa regime inherited an inflation rate that rose 586% in 1990 after a perilous increase in 1989, reason enough to free prices in order to bring goods to the market. The overwhelming foreign debt was approaching default, threatening financial panic. The country, in the opinion of Jeffrey Sachs, fresh from Harvard on the scene as a Walesa advisor, "was a basket case." Balcerowicz states he avoided the term in public statements because of its emotional content, exploited by opponents in the gradualist camp. If shock treatment means a comprehensive, radical package rather than gradual change, Balcerowicz as psychologist says so be it. The transition authorities have only a brief honeymoon, when people will act "in the common good," before reverting to personal or sectoral interests, such as unions preoccupied with more wages. The costs of administering incremental deregulation are much higher for a strapped government, and the risks greater. Besides, each of the transition strategies reenforces the other, and should not be delayed. For example, promoting exports applies pressure against the prevailing substitution of imports for goods that should be produced at home in response to higher prices.

* * *

Jeffrey Sachs, writing five years after Poland's "shock therapy," offers his usual broad analysis, first, of the conceptual basis leading to the program, and then an evaluation of results, in contrast to Balcerowicz's pragmatic, put-out-the fire procedure. First, he emphasizes the radical program must be seen in the context of a world economy committed to integration and interdependence, through networks of production, finance, and a shared acknowledgment of capitalism as the normal system. No country in the advanced world can risk not joining up. For a transition country in Eastern Europe, the only choice is to look outward, in this case to Western Europe. Going slowly meant missing out on markets, and losing foreign investments from other countries and regions already in pursuit of the prize.

Additionally there was no way to learn the strategies and techniques of global capitalism without entering the fray. The objective for Poland was a "return to Europe" as soon as possible, a goal, he states, that was endorsed by Solidarity and the important Polish media.

Sachs laments in retrospect that the idea of a jump-start, which he publicized, implied instant accomplishment. No such result was possible after forty-five years as a Soviet-distorted economy. The financial crisis might subside quickly, as it did in Poland's "life and death battle against inflation and default on debts." But the long-term adjustment in changing from the Soviet system of central planning and state ownership is another matter. In that sense, the metaphor is misleading; it only gives the patient a fresh opportunity that will take years, perhaps decades, to come into fruition. Still, he praises Poland's success in taking to a market-economy "like a fish to water." Hundreds of thousands of new businesses, especially in the new services sectors; over two-thirds of the work force in the private sector; over two million private businesses. True, there is poverty and high unemployment, but the latter is overstated because of the gray market, and is in line with Western European averages.[13] To his credit, Sachs has always included a mandate for social relief in his strategy agendas; yet he generally overlooks this concern in ensuing evaluations.

* * *

So much for shock therapy: how it worked and how it promised too much. The Polish and Czech successes, however, leave a problem about Russia's same strategy and failed results. The usual explanations are as one would expect: too large a country; too long under Communism; too weak the presidential powers; too much crime and corruption; too little tax collection; too little and too late foreign aid; too large an entrenched bureaucracy in 18,000 larger firms; too large an army. If we start at the end of ten years, however, with Russia's misery index, and its pension and payroll arrearages, a strong case can be made for gradualism rather than shock therapy.

Notes

1 See Ivan Berend, *Central Europe and Eastern Europe 1944–1993, detour from the periphery* (London: Cambridge University Press, 1996). In Berend's view, the post-Communist transformation in Eastern Europe is closely related to the countries' repeated efforts to come to terms with their peripheral position regarding Western Europe.

2 Václav Klaus, "The Czech Exception," *New Perspectives Quarterly*, Spring 1996, 12.

3 The dissenter's voice on Hungarian success is strongly heard from Ivan Berend (see Note 1 *supra*). His credentials as Hungarian historian and witness are exemplary. He spent his fourteenth birthday in 1944 in prison during the fascist regime of Admiral Horthy. He was instrumental in the belated honoring of Imre Nagy and the 1956 uprising. In 1989, he headed a privatization and marketing committee during the final period of "reform-revolution," preceding Russia's "velvet-revolution" exit. Now Professor of History at UCLA, and Director of Russian and Eastern European Studies, he served in 1989–1993 on an international advisory committee for Hungary's transition. For him, the "Annus Mirabilis" of 1989 for Hungary has been followed by "Anni Miserabiles," marked by severe "destruction" of gross domestic product, poverty, unemployment, sellout of industries to foreign companies, and mindless submission to market-economy objectives, imposed for the most part by the foreign-aid agencies, that offset all the good statistics. (See Berend, *Central Europe*, 1996, 341–363.) His claims seem one-sided for 1994, and difficult to sustain for 1997.

4 The importance of becoming an export country is tied to the effort to stop import substitution of goods better made in the home country. For transition countries, new foreign markets were also needed to replace the collapsed Soviet-group of trading partners (CMEA or Council for Mutual Economic Assistance). For more on exports, see Jeffrey D. Sachs and Andrew Warner, "Economic Reform and the Process of Global Integration," (Brookings Papers on Economic Activity, I, 1995, Washington, DC). 57–63, in which the authors, starting from their concept of the all-embracing, peacetime global-capitalist interdependence of foreign trade, claim that those who join up will prosper, while others will fail. They produce statistics to show that only the strong trade-reformers in the transition countries (e.g., Hungary, Poland and the Czech Republic) have

shown good GDP growth by 1994. They caution that more tests of this hypothesis will require a longer time-period.

5 International Monetary Fund, *World Economic Outlook*, May 1977, 108.

6 Leszek Balcerowicz, *Socialism, Capitalism, Transformation* (Budapest: Central University Press, 1995), 369.

7 Balcerowicz, *Socialism*, 356–57.

8 Balcerowicz, *Socialism*, 362–63.

9 Layard, *Coming Russian Boom*, 361.

10 Mario I. Blejer and Fabrizio Coricelli, *The Making of Economic Reform in Eastern Europe* (Aldershot, UK: Edward Elgar, 1995), 16–18.

11 Balcerowicz, *Socialism*, 362.

12 Irving S. Michelman, *The Moral Limitations of Capitalism* (Aldershot, UK: Avebury, 1994), 148–50.

13 See Jeffrey Sachs, "Shock Therapy in Poland: Perspectives of Five Years," Tanner Lectures on Human Values, University of Utah, April 1994. Sachs is the virtuoso of advisors to post-Communist transition governments, among others Poland, 1989–91, Yugoslavia, 1989–90, Slovenia, 1991, and Russia, 1991–94. Anders Åslund, influential advisor to Russia from Stockholm, regarded as the leading authority and historian of Russia's transition, says of Sachs: "...our undisputed intellectual leader. In any situation, he can conceptualize the problems, structure them, and immediately propose viable solutions." (*How Russia Became a Market Economy*, 1995, xi.) Within the home front, the resident economists are less generous. Leszek Balcerowicz confines acknowledgement of Sachs to a brief footnote in *Capitalism, Socialism, Transformation*.

5 Privatization: The Defining Strategy of Transition

The defining strategy of the march to capitalism in the transition countries is privatization, the change from state-ownership to private ownership, or at least achieving major, irreversible steps in that direction. All the other strategies, the freeing of prices and currency, the curbing of state expenditures to match income, the reduction of subsidies to industry and individuals, and the turn to international trade, all these pale by comparison. Without privatization there is no change in system, no transition.

In Russia's case there is a further complication. Capitalism, the great diffuser of property to the masses, is the newcomer on the block. Historically property ownership in Western civilization has been for the few, the imperial families, the universal church, feudal barons, and, finally, monarchs and their aristocrats and oligarchs. When modern democracy inaugurated an end to such exclusive control of economic power in the name of liberty, inspiring Adam Smith to call his theoretical construct "a system of natural liberty," to reflect its freedom factor, Russia was not impressed. Its end-stage of state-capitalism was reasonably effective, but only as the agent for autocratic czars and aristocrats, intent on maintaining a tight hold on property. Historians are no longer surprised at Russia's turn to Communism, reversing Marx's prediction, when they note Russia's age-old tradition of state-owned and controlled property, and its philosophical obsession with utopianism.

* * *

Such thoughts aside, how do we measure Russia's success with privatization in the last decade of the twentieth century? As frequently happens with maximum change, the process can be viewed in two stages.

The first stage, 1992–1994, witnessed a remarkable and successful transfer of ownership in terms of quantity. Its distinguishing feature could well be the audacity of its execution, but it did not spring entirely from the brows of its executioners. Gorbachev had already opened the door to privatization, as he did for so much of the transition, before being deposed by his radical rival Yeltsin.

The chronology of Russia's transition shows that as early as November 1986, Gorbachev, a year after his incredibly agile act of becoming general secretary of the unsuspecting USSR's Communist Party, succeeding Chernenko in 1985, ushered through a Law on Individual Labor and Activity, allowing some enterprise at innocuous levels. In 1988 further laws allowed cooperatives to act as enterprises and permitted the sale of state-owned apartments to individuals. One might ask why buy when you have bargain rent-control, but 10,000 apartments were purchased that year, and by the end of 1990, 53,000 apartments and 4,432 family farms had been privatized,[1] while hundreds of thousands, some say millions, still retained their tiny, produce-producing countryside *dachas*, not swept into the state.

Now starts a paper-chase of high-level commissions and proposals that foundered on Gorbachev's uncertainty, the crumbling of the empire, economic distress, strikes, and the implacable ambition of Yeltsin, who had been humiliated and cast out of Gorbachev's Politboro in 1987, over differences about reform. In 1989, Gorbachev created a Commission on Economic Reform under Deputy Prime Minister Abalkin that presented a program embracing an important segment of market economy, the freeing of prices, convertible currency, and even a stock exchange. It was dead-on-arrival, as was a similar plan presented by Gorbachev's liberal economist Grigory Yavlinsky. These plans for market and property reforms became a matter of political rivalry as Yeltsin in effect established his own shadow government in Russia, where he had become Chairman of its newly-decentralized government, challenging the sovereignty of the Soviet superstructure. Yavlinsky had opportunely defected to become a Yeltsin deputy prime minister, and the plans flew once again. In August 1990, a new group of economists under Stanislav Shatalin, with Yavlinsky's aid, convened by the estranged Gorbachev and Yeltsin, produced still another 500-day plan for economic reform. Yeltsin's Supreme Soviet (then the name of Russia's legislature) approved the Shatalin Plan by a 213 to 1 vote, but Gorbachev unwisely rejected it for the USSR. The deadly game continued with Yeltsin demanding Gorbachev's resignation on TV in February 1991, while defiantly producing tentative laws for housing and privatization of state enterprises for Russia, the heartland of the Union. Gorbachev then played his final card in the reform sweepstakes by decreeing some privatization, never effected, for the entire USSR, while on his well-known vacation in Foros, near the Black Sea, scene of the infamous putsch of August 19–21, 1991. The putsch played into Yeltsin's hands and enabled full-blown privatization to become a reality in Russia the next year.

* * *

In June 1991 Yeltsin established his legitimacy in Russia by becoming its first freely-elected sovereign in 1,000 years, elected as president by a 57.3% vote, enabling him to launch a new reform program. On October 28, 1991, aware that Russia's chaotic economy was threatened with free-fall, Yeltsin made what Anders Åslund terms a "great speech on radical economic reform" to Russia's Congress of People's Deputies. The essence of the speech was to seize the moment for thorough and decisive economic reforms. Russia's trouble was never a shortage of reformers and their plans, he said, but instead an inability to be consistent and decisive, in short a plea for shock treatment. A fundamental changeover was the only option left. His legislators were aware that Poland had chosen an apparently successful shock program in early 1990, and in January 1991, the less-threatened Czechoslovakia had followed suit. "I appeal to you at one of the most critical moments of Russian history. Right now it will be decided what kind of country Russia will be in the coming years and decades." The period of small steps is over, he said, and a big reformist breakthrough is necessary. Although the speech mentioned concrete measures about prices, financial stabilization, and privatization, the unspoken words about privatization were the tremendous consequences it involved. In his 1994 memoirs, Yeltsin relates his commitment to break the Communist stronghold on the economy through privatization:

> There was probably no other way to do it. Except for Stalinist industry, adapted to modern conditions and a Stalinist economy, no other industry existed here. Just as it had been created, so must it be destroyed.[2]

* * *

The agents of destruction were a youthful, open-minded economist, Yegor Gaidar, and his friend, the equally youthful and unknown Deputy Mayor of St. Petersburg, Anatoly Chubais, also an economist. It is a mark of Yeltsin's genius that he frequently tapped such outstanding talent in the midst of his perilous administration, often against the advice of foreign advisors and international-aid officials.

A flashback to the ubiquitous advisors will set the stage for the rise of Gaidar and the subsequent first-stage privatization efforts of Chubais, in the center again of Russian life as a first-deputy prime minister in Yeltsin's present administration. The Swedish diplomat and economist Anders Åslund arrived in Russia a few weeks after the failed August 1991 coup, convinced that the Russian government would secede from the USSR and would be in great need for advice on radical and comprehensive market reforms, similar to Poland's experience after the Solidarity triumph in 1990. Jeffrey Sachs of Harvard, his antennae alerted, also arrived in Moscow at the same time and for the same purpose. Åslund returned to Moscow in September to meet with a promising Yeltsin deputy prime minister, one Yevgeny Saburov, but lost interest when the latter expressed a preference for gradualism. At the airport, headed for Stockholm, he met an old friend from his various European conferences, Aleksandr Shokhin, then Yeltsin's minister of labor. Shokhin told him about a group led by Yegor Gaidar and others who had given up on Gorbachev and were opting for a new program and administration for Russia, with Gaidar potential deputy prime minister for economic policy.

The group was meeting regularly at a *dacha* in Arkhangelskoe, on the outskirts of Moscow, in contact with Yeltsin via his confidante, Gennady Burbulis. Åslund signed up for himself and Sachs, agreeing that their presence should be submerged until the politically-correct moment. Åslund recalls that he had long-hoped that an under-forty generation of economists, relatively independent of Communist ideology, would emerge as a brain-trust for radical reforms, replacing the older generation of reformers like Abalkin and Shatalin. By 1988 the door had been opened by Gorbachev, and young economists were travelling abroad. At one such meeting in Hungary in the spring of 1988, attendees included Anatoly Chubais, Leszek Balcerowicz, and Václav Klaus, all destined to guide their countries economically in the near future.[3] Åslund knew Chubais from foreign conferences, but not Gaidar until Åslund lectured at Gaidar's Institute of Economic Policy in June 1991, only a few months before the putsch. From 1987 on, Åslund had been reading Gaidar's venturesome but guarded articles in the journal *Kommunist*. He was heartened to learn Gaidar had assembled an ideal group for a new government.[4]

* * *

More about Yeltsin's subversive economist: Yegor Gaidar came from a family of Soviet literary elite. His father was a rear-admiral and prominent journalist who had been a foreign correspondent for *Pravda*. Accordingly Yegor lived in Cuba and Yugoslavia until high-school graduation. He graduated from Moscow University's Department of Economics with honors. For a time, he worked on the Party's journal *Kommunist* and as an economics editor for *Pravda*, acquiring a PhD and a family by the time Yeltsin drafted him at the age of thirty-five. Yeltsin had not met him until he bravely rallied to Yeltsin's side on the first day of the attempted coup, August 19, 1991. Gaidar, in a later article, recalled his predicament when Yeltsin summoned him to become economic czar and lightening-rod for the reform government:

> I could have given a perfect explanation of why in 1992 reforms should not have been launched...no stable support in the parliament. No normal functions of government (army, customs, police)...sixteen

central banks instead of one...no traditions of enterprise, or private sector, as in Poland...not a kopeck of hard currency or gold reserves... no hope of foreign investment...But we couldn't wait any longer.[5]

Gaidar lasted only thirteen months on the job, sacrificed, as noted in chapter 1, to placate Yeltsin's turncoat parliament as the honeymoon period ended. Chernomyrdin and other conservative-appearing bureaucrats were appointed to fill the breach. Meanwhile, Gaidar and his team had resolutely launched reforms on all fronts. Above all, he worked with Chubais to ride the momentum and inaugurate the epic wave of privatization that would constitute an irreversible path to transition.

Inevitably Gaidar would earn both criticism and praise from outside authorities on such matters. Marshall Goldman, expert on the Soviet Union and associate director of Russian Studies at Harvard, is not a Gaidar fan. He regards the early shock-therapy program of Yeltsin and Gaidar as no better than Gorbachev's indecision, with more serious results. On the scene in Russia at the time, he felt Gaidar was over his head, without practical experience, and lacking in empathy for potential economic victims. He could understand why Aleksandr Rutskoi, Yeltsin's disloyal vice-president, and similar politicians could not relate to the young theorist.[6]

Anders Åslund, ensconced from December 1991 to March 1993 in the former Communist Party headquarters, close to the Kremlin, with Sachs, Layard, Marek Dobrowski of Poland, and other foreign advisors, has a different impression. He expresses his admiration for Gaidar, Chubais, and Federov, "the men behind the great transformation to a market economy." Gaidar stands out, he says, as the most competent economist to have served in the Russian government, with proven ability to conceptualize a program and implement it with considerable decisiveness. Even in his brief return to government from September 1993 to January 1994, in the constant musical chairs of Russian politics, Åslund feels Gaidar facilitated substantial reforms.[7]

Finally, a word from the durable Yeltsin. President Bush phoned him, he writes in his memoirs, to keep Gaidar when parliament was demanding his head, as the West saw him as the guarantor of economic reforms, but he knew it was time to appoint Chernomyrdin as prime minister as a matter of expediency. He had chosen Gaidar as architect of reform very carefully, he writes, "impressed most of all with his confidence...he was an independent man with an enormous sense of his own worth, a member of the intelligentsia, who, unlike the dull bureaucrats in the government administration, would not hide his opinions...he would fight for his own principles to the end." Besides, "he had a knack for speaking simply," a quality not easy to find in economists wherever one happens to live.[8] Some might see a mirror-image in Yeltsin's recollections. They remind us that in the country that once sponsored a materialist-determination of history, men, not matters alone, make history. In that mode we can visit Anatoly Chubais and his privatization program.

* * *

The great achievement of the first stage of privatization was overcoming opposition in the Russian parliament towards such a fundamental change. This was a period of increasing conservative, populist and nationalist dissent, amidst inflation that refused to subside. It is symbolized by Yeltsin, the heroic figure standing on a tank to quell the coup against Gorbachev in August 1991, finally shelling his own parliament, after it refused his order for dissolution, on October 3, 1993. In that roiling period, enough to try men's souls for democracy, let alone capitalism, the Speaker of the parliament, Ruslan Khasbulatov, himself a former reform-economist, was a constant thorn. He demanded a return to price controls on April 2, 1992, and asked his legislators to impeach Yeltsin on March 28, 1993, reminiscent of Yeltsin's own demands on Gorbachev in February 1991. With Yeltsin's Vice President Aleksandr Rutskoi, a former general, the parliamentarian rebels initiated a minor armed-uprising and occupied the parliament. They named Rutskoi president for a day, until escorted to jail themselves. Yeltsin covered his tracks by promising and delivering a new election and constitution, thereby restoring the legitimacy, but not the safe-conduct, of his administration. Most historians believe Yeltsin survived that period not for his reforms, but as a lesser evil than the old type of government, even more disliked and distrusted by the newly-enfranchised voters.

* * *

The selected privatization strategy was a massive redistribution of the shares of state-owned enterprises as soon as possible. Did the reformers consider other alternatives? The best argument for gradualism, such as the deliberate, costly, case-by-case appraisal and sale of medium and larger enterprises in Hungary, would be the time gained for establishing the supporting framework of capitalism in Russia. These would include capitalism's proven ground-rules, reliable corporation and contract laws, legislation allowing management to lay off excessive employees, bankruptcy procedures to weed out the thousands of money-losers, a sound tax-system, perhaps anti-monopoly statutes, and certainly securities legislation for the new class of shareholders, all waiting to be taught and financed by an avalanche of foreign-aid professionals. Gaidar, Chubais, and Yeltsin thought otherwise, and not, as may be charged, as believers in unfettered capitalism. Considering the political context in parliament, and pre-conditions in Russia, few can second-guess them. For privatization to occur in Russia, the time-factor was essential: privatization first, institutions second. Gaidar and Chubais acknowledged that their own time was limited politically, and proceeded accordingly.

* * *

How did Chubais keep one step ahead of parliament and place Russia irretrievably on the road to capitalism? In June 1992, after Yeltsin's preliminary announcement endorsing the program, Chubais convinced parliamentary leaders to let him engage in a major privatization plan by the end of the year that would distribute vouchers exchangeable for share ownership in a large number of industrial firms. The vouchers would go first to employees and managers, and then to the public at large. There were trade-offs and tactics behind Chubais's unexpected victory. For example, the government accepted defeat on a concurrent request to permit increased privatization of state-owned land. Chubais also gained favorable attention in the media, where the newly-freed editors and reporters were generally on the side of reform. The idea of something for nothing in the form of tangible, attractive voucher-certificates, to be made available to every citizen in Russia, including children, created great interest among families accustomed to life-long queues before official desks, waiting for rubber-stamped permits. Hungary's previous attempt at small-scale voucher distributions upon written application won little success. It was a lesson learned, as was Czechoslovakia's ongoing success with a small country's use of privatization-vouchers. Implicit to the whole project was the lure of future profits, in keeping with the capitalist scenario.

There were other factors coming to Chubais's aid. First, some of the parliamentary opposition were caught off-guard, assuming the grandiose program would be sabotaged by the reliable bureaucracy, or self-destructed by Yeltsin's ouster in the six remaining months of preparation. Also the industry giants like Gazprom were placed far on the agenda, with promises that 40% or more of their shares would be retained by the state. Railways, defense, health and education would not be privatized. The basic tactic, however, was Chubais's upping the ante for the percentage of vouchers to be offered first to employees and management, retaining only 29% of the shares for the public.

A true capitalist approach would go to the public first with a majority of the vouchers in order to avoid a repetition of entrenched management, able to induce employees to vote on its behalf, and remaining immune from outside shareholders. On the other hand, the awarding of a large portion of the shares to employees and middle-managers resonated with Marx's distant call for workers to own the forces of production. High-level managers and industry-ministers also figured they might become rich as well as powerful in the new dispensation. Finally, Yeltsin used his decree powers to implement the program whenever possible. The vouchers themselves rested on such a decree.

Until Chubais writes his own memoirs, much of the political transactions will remain unknown. Two American professors-on-leave, along with a Russian counterpart, Maxim Boycko, have been acknowledged by Chubais as his "closest advisors." They return the compliment in their book on that period: "The parliamentary battles that surrounded the adoption of the program...were fought and won by Chubais."[9]

* * *

Voucher Capitalism

The Polish experiment with vouchers established about twenty mutual funds, managed by foreign investment bankers like Goldman Sachs and Morgan Grenfell, to administer shares in 400 selected industrial firms. The investment bankers, acting more or less as trustees for a management fee, were to watch out for their new shareholders. Each Polish citizen was given a share in each of the twenty funds, in effect becoming a shareholder in twenty groups of assorted companies. The 400 state-firms were now in the hands of the fund-managers, representing millions of citizen shareholders, who could keep or trade their fund shares as they wished. The funds would eventually stay in this role, or buy shares for their own account, or liquidate by going public with their companies, or otherwise distributing to their shareholders, all in good capitalist fashion.

The Polish approach emphasized good corporate governance as the strategic objective, rather than getting rid of controlling politicians, the overriding goal of Chubais and his group, who spoke continuously of "de-politicalizing" the Russian economy. The group could not conceive of "some 35-year old British or American investment banker telling a Polish [i.e. Russian] manager to sack 3,000 people without this manager calling some minister or legislator demanding that the foreigner be ignored."[10] In their belief, short of exiling the entrenched politicians and bureaucrats, whom they believed to be the absolute source of Russia's inefficiency and stagnation, the preferred strategy was to establish an unorganized majority of employees, managers, local governments, and the public as the new shareholders. This would leave the government functionaries hanging in the wind, somewhat like Gorbachev without the Communist Party and the Soviet Union superstructure. There was also a difference in scale, with about 20,000 medium and large-sized firms to be privatized.

This theory should not go unchallenged. Most of Russia's vast planning and distribution ministries were dissolved without much difficulty in the early days of Yeltsin's reform. Much of the essential disbursements of funds to industry were curbed when the central bank yielded to reforms by Boris Federov, minister of finance and deputy prime minister in 1993. Prime Minister Chernomyrdin, the epitome of the political-bureaucrat, railed against privatization upon taking office, but quickly came around to strong support for Chubais's mandate. There was enough opposition to Yeltsin from nationalists, populists, the military, and other rivals, without making de-politicalization the overwhelming goal of privatization, at the expense of better corporate governance. It is something of a scapegoat theory. Privatization itself takes the state out of industry. Additionally, the Communist Party, for generations in charge of industry, had been effectively removed from the picture by Yeltsin at the outset of his regime.

Meanwhile, Poland has done very well. It is the leader in sustained growth of gross domestic product. It has produced over 800,000 new business enterprises, and its variety of privatization programs has resulted in over 70% of its GDP in the private sector. In July 1997, the investment funds, holding 10% of Poland's GDP, successfully completed their five-year program by going public with the state-owned companies, on Poland's own Stock Exchange, at market prices.

What cannot be challenged is the Chubais team's awareness of public psychology in Russia. There would first of all be intense nationalist rejection of foreign-fund managers. Second, they determined a noticeable lack of appeal in Poland for vouchers attached at the outset to sober funds, compared with the great enthusiasm for the Czech vouchers, which were carefully explained in advance travels by the astute Václav Klaus.[11] Czech vouchers were promoted as a return of personal property, with complete freedom to use them for buying company shares, if an employee, to sell them to aggressive funds, or to wait for voucher-auctions. The Chubais program adopted these features and added a further choice. The Russian vouchers were not only denominated in cash (10,000 rubles, or about $80), as the Czech vouchers were not, but they could also be freely traded, despite the great risk of price fluctuations, adding to the constant talk about vouchers.[12] The Russians have demonstrated a pent-up desire for choice. This is evidenced by their numerous political parties and wide-ranging media, their propensity to vote in large numbers, their turn to diverse religions, their moral ambiguity about millionaires, Mafia, and corruption, and, for many, their conspicuous consumption.

* * *

Between October 1992 and January 1993, about 140 million vouchers had been picked up at the thousands of State Savings Banks offices. The final voucher-auctions of shares to outsiders were held in June 1994. In that last opportunity to get under the wire, 3,000 firms completed their privatization to the public, including Gazprom and some of Russia's largest firms in telecommunications, oil, and non-ferrous metals. Altogether 14,000 sizeable industrial firms completed their auctions in twenty months. Over 600 mutual funds had been formed in this period. They exchanged their own shares for 45 million vouchers and were dominant at the auctions.

The share price for the so-called auctions was the original 1.7 times low book-value, unrelated to present or future earnings, established by the firms themselves, guided by the privatization ministry earlier in the process for sale of shares to workers and managers. The bargain prices were maintained at the auctions, with shares allocated to buyers in proportion to the vouchers submitted. The outside shares, however, never reached the Yeltsin-approved 29%, capping at only 18%. Still, it was a major technical feat in a turbulent political period, and generally free of manipulation, other than shameless understating of book-value on the part of industry giants like Gazprom, and VAZ, Russia's largest auto manufacturer, for the benefit of insiders. It was accomplished by an outstanding team of economists, with the aid of foreign advisors and considerable financing from the foreign-aid agencies.

* * *

Boycko, Shleifer, and Vishny rightly take pride in their hands-on account of Russia's unprecedented peacetime economic transformation. Besides the demonization of the already-doomed industry-ministers, fighting a last-ditch struggle for their turf, however, there are additional disconcerting claims. They make the claim, often repeated, that Russia now has 40 million future capital-ists, more shareholders than in any similar part of the world, due to their shares in industry and voucher-funds.[13] They ingenuously quote the remark of Brian Atwood, head of the US Agency for International Development, visiting a bakery-auction in Moscow: "the first place he saw where capitalism actually worked."[14] Suffice to say voucher-capitalism was indeed effective but not substantive, a quick strike to end a reeling state-ownership system. Capitalism is a lengthy, organic process of rights and responsibilities, taxes and benefits, that is not easily won. The 400,000 coal-miners described in chapter 4 cannot be enthused about owning shares in their obsolete, non-competitive mines. They want their pay, including back pay, and look to the state to hasten or at least ameliorate the process.

Similarly, the claims for irreversibility might rest on more persuasive grounds:

> ...cancelling the program would have constituted confiscation of people's assets. The government became a hostage of vouchers...and could only reverse the program at a prohibitive political cost.[15]

Russia's commitment is to democracy as well as to capitalism. Insuring a democratic government by holding it hostage to voucher-expropriation is a slender reed for guarding democracy. Democracies like France and England have nationalized and de-nationalized major industries without fanfare. In fact, a rational theory of growth for developing countries might include fostering state-owned industries such as airlines, telecommunications, and the like, before privatizing them at immense profits, as an approved formula. If Russia's capitalism is irreversible in the long-run, it will be because it is democratically-chosen and works for the benefit of most people.

The Second Stage

A story as momentous as the privatization of a superpower resists closure. The major sequence of the post-voucher phase is the ongoing privatization of industry giants, selling their shares, still minority allotments, at market prices to the highest bidder, foreign or domestic. A typical 1997 development is the sale of shares in the telecommunications giant AO Svyazinvest, bidding to start at $1.18 billion for a 25% share. This is far more than Gazprom's breakthrough sale of 1.15% of its shares for $415 million in October 1996.

The billion-dollar sale is important for Russia's cash-starved budget, as the foreign-aid agencies are likely to keep two sets of books, one that includes such proceeds as deficit-reduction items, while Russia is still struggling for economic survival. Additionally the proceeds are non-inflationary, and will create desperately-needed employment and future taxes. From the point of view of corporate governance, the holders of 25% will not easily be dissuaded by entrenched management, or by other elements, currently corrupt interlopers rather than the previously-feared industry-ministers and *nomenklatura*. Large investors, mostly institutional, will not be deterred from their objective of an efficient and profitable operation. The fact that prestigious international bankers will participate in the bidding is also significant. Such managers, although not underwriting the issue, stand ready to pick up the shares in the resale market, since they lay their reputations on the line in relation to accounting standards, taxes, political risk, and similar representations.

This large distribution to the public also sets the tone for a new standard in the country's second-stage privatization program. There had been a series of bitterly-criticized sales, including major companies, where buyers, often Russia's speculating banks, would buy shares on time, secured by the shares themselves, with the government in the position of having to reclaim the shares in case of default. The owners might scramble to sell off the shares to other purchasers to avoid default, but it was not a preferred way to privatize, leading to scandals about rigged prices, insider deals, and accusations of monopoly. Inevitably charges of creating a Big Seven type of oligarchy, reminiscent of South Korean and Japanese combines, have been raised about these often predatory acquisitors. Again there is a redemptive feature in such concentrated ownership. Large investors at least do not want to lose their capital. Also such combinations will yield to a turn to regulated capitalism, under government surveillance, when they go too far.

Back to Svyazinvest. A previous attempt to sell the 25% stake in 1995 failed. An Italian communications giant won the bidding but backed off over technicalities. In its new role as a share-selling candidate, seeking to raise a large cash infusion for improving operations, Svyazinvest merged with the state-controlled Russian long-distance monopoly. With its own 25 million access-lines, and a long-distance operation as well, its shares became marketable at a premium price. The expected bidders include Deutsche Telekom and perhaps ATT.

This type of encouraging news is supplemented by a steady stream in 1997 of other public offerings and international borrowings, along with co-ventures as varied as a deal with China for billions to be spent on building energy pipelines. It is difficult to look back at the early '90s, when privatizing apartments, some farm collectives, and turning over small shops and services to their state-managers, was an important step forward. By the end of 1995, there were 17,937 medium and large-sized privatized enterprises, and 12,118,000 privatized apartments, according to the figures now supplied by a revived corps of Russian statistical bureaus. For those who see significance in new business starts, (family businesses account for 50% of America's GDP), the statisticians report 794,000 new businesses have been started in Russia during the transition period.[16] Poland claims a substantially larger number, with only 25% of Russia's population.[17]

Notes

1 Joseph R. Blasi, Maya Kroumova, and Douglas Kruse, *Kremlin Capitalism* (Ithaca, NY: Cornell University Press, 1997), xv.

2 Yeltsin, *Struggle for Russia*, 200.

3 Goldman, *Lost Opportunity*, 88.

4 Åslund, *How Russia Became a Market Economy*, 18–19.

5 Yeltsin, *Struggle for Russia*, 156.

6 Goldman, *Lost Opportunity*, 90–93.

7 Åslund, *How Russian Became a Market Economy*, xi, 315.

8 Yeltsin, *Struggle for Russia*, 125.

9 Maxim Boycko, Andrei Shleifer, Robert Vishny, *Privatizing Russia* (Cambridge: MIT Press, 1995), 3. Shleifer was on leave from Harvard,

and Vishny from University of Chicago. In 1997, Shleifer ended his work in Russia when the US AID program withdrew funding over an alleged conflict of interest.

10 Boycko, *Privatizing Russia*, 83.

11 The Czechoslovakian government offered 11 million adults the right to buy a voucher book for a nominal fee of $36 in 1992. As a result, 8.6 million books were purchased for a total of $310 million. Since the book value of the selected 2,000 state enterprises to be privatized was announced to be $9.3 billion, visions of huge profits were generated. Unregulated investment funds, over 80 of which became listed on the revived Prague Stock Exchange, started saturation-advertising, many guaranteeing a 10 for 1 profit, gathering a large amount of vouchers. The government belatedly restricted the funds from such potential deception (letter to author from Prague Stock Exchange, 9 October 1996). This casual laissez-faire attitude to financial institutions boomeranged for the otherwise competent Václav Klaus. In 1997, a series of major banks and investment funds tumbled over charges of fraud, excessive fees, inside deals, and embezzlement. An estimated 700,000 or 7% of the population claim they lost their investments in the funds. There is considerable loss-control in that the vouchers, unlike Russia's, were not tradeable, so individual losses were minimal. Also, government had retained a large portion of its key industries for later direct privatization. Still the pain and scandal threatened the long-running Klaus regime.

12 See Boycko, *Privatizing Russia*, 86, 101–102. Voucher prices dropped as low as $5.00 in April 1993 and rose to about $23 in June 1994. At time of issue to each family member at 10,000 rubles, then worth $80, the average monthly wage was $50.

13 Boycko, *Privatizing Russia*, 148, 151.

14 Boycko, *Privatizing Russia*, 108.

15 Boycko, *Privatizing Russia*, 84.

16 Blasi, *Kremlin Capitalism*, xix.

17 Poland is also a leading client for Daewoo, the unpredictable South Korean conglomerate that is aggressively investing throughout the former Soviet bloc. Daewoo has announced $2 billion for co-venturing auto production in Poland, mostly on pledges, but some projects are well underway. Hungary, the Czech Republic, and Russia to date hold little interest for Daewoo.

6 Gorbachev's Economic Reforms

Gorbachev is now a voice from the past in Russia's turbulent transition, particularly in regard to economic reform. All the great moves, the effective ending of Communist Party involvement in the economy, the shock-treatment of price and currency deregulation, the commitment to the market system, the opening-up of foreign trade, the ending of state subsidies under the prodding of the foreign-aid agencies, and the irreversible privatization of enterprise, occurred on Yeltsin's watch.

Yet Gorbachev will go down in history as a great man. Before reviewing his failed economic efforts, we should give credit where it is due. Consider the following from Archie Brown, Gorbachev's English biographer:

> Gorbachev has strong claims to be regarded as the individual who made the most profound impact on history in the second half of the twentieth century. He played the decisive part in allowing the countries of Eastern Europe to become free and independent. He did more than anyone else to end the Cold War between East and West...He initiated radically new thinking about the political and economic system he inherited...and presided over the introduction of freedom of speech, freedom of association, religious freedom, and freedom of movement.[1]

Brown, strongly biased towards his subject, helped brief Prime Minister Thatcher in 1984 when Gorbachev boldly led a parliamentary delegation to visit England, while a favorite candidate to succeed the ailing Chernenko. Thatcher announced "they could do business together," and conveyed her sentiments to President Reagan, who later concluded missiles and nuclear disarmament proposals initiated by Gorbachev. A look at Gorbachev taking his first salute on the Kremlin reviewing stand in November 1985 suggests the maze he had entered. Surrounded by a gerontocracy of unsmiling Andrei Gromyko-prototypes, the handsome, unlined general secretary is characteristically self-confident. His arch-enemy, Boris Yeltsin, to this day unable to say anything complimentary about Gorbachev, who shares the feeling, comes right to the pòint:

> The chief problem of [Gorbachev's] launching of *perestroika* was that he was practically alone, surrounded by the authors and impresarios of Brezhnev's 'era of stagnation,' who were determined to ensure the indestructibility of the old order of things. After a while, it became easier for him, and then he himself began to lag behind events. But at that all important initial moment of his reforming initiative, he operated with amazing finesse. In no way did he frighten the old mafia of the Party *apparat*, which retained its form a long time and which, if necessary, might have eaten any general secretary alive without so much as a hiccup.[2]

In fairness to Gorbachev, Communist Party power over both state and economy was substantially reduced under his leadership, facilitating the lethal blow by Yeltsin after the coup, which involved high Party officials in its leadership. In July 1988, Gorbachev decentralized the Party administration and reduced its staff. In May 1989, after his almost freely-elected Congress of Peoples Deputies designated him president, according to plan, the Congress then repealed the Constitutional Article specifying a "leading role" for the Party. The Politboro was replaced by a President's Council in 1990, and the powerful Party Central Committee ceased to meet. As an exercise in *glasnost*, Gorbachev put the Congress on TV from 1989 on, adding to the Party's visible disrepute. Membership, only ten per cent of the adult population to start with, fell by the millions. All in all, in a belated attempt to gain a more legitimate, non-Party basis for his administration, Gorbachev instigated the end of the Party that had nourished him and brought him to power. Ironically, he remained general secretary of the Party as well as president of the Soviet Union until the end.

* * *

Why review Gorbachev's failures on the economic side? First, historical figures are defined by their failures as well as successes, particularly when the failures have historical consequences. Gorbachev's unsuccessful attempts at economic reform gave the Yeltsin regime the opportunity to end the system at any cost. Second, there is the fundamental ideological dilemma faced by Gorbachev and his close advisors. Should the administration endeavor to produce a reformed-version of socialism or cross the line to the market-system, with its promises of prosperity and obvious relationship with democracy, not to mention billions from foreign-aid agencies. There are claims for socialism far-removed from the shattering totalitarian excesses of Stalin, and now Lenin. They include, among others, biblical injunctions, ideal utopias, the intellectual proposals of Shaw and the Fabians in England, the Depression-born versions of Norman Thomas and Reinhold Niebuhr in America, and the Swedish middle-way.[3] Their implicit legacies are found in the budgets of any advanced capitalist country, 25% to 30% for so-called social benefits. The intensity of devoted adherents like Gorbachev cannot be dismissed. Finally, there is the need to evaluate Gorbachev and Yeltsin in their present roles as the century ends.

* * *

No End of Proposals

There was no lack of economic proposals on the desk of Gorbachev, a highly-trained technocrat at home with reorganization plans, consolidations of committees, statistics, five-year plans (as against the 500-day plan of the Yeltsin group, the rejection of which would accelerate his downfall), and demands for worker discipline, in short, a preference for management objectives rather than radical reform. There were considerable accomplishments, for example, a reduction in the Soviet ministries, largely economic, from 2.4 million to 1.6 million in the first few years of his administration.[4] The overall economic results were dismal from the start, however, aggravated by a reduction in world energy prices, affecting the bail-out traditionally flowing to Russia from its natural resources. The economy was further stricken by Gorbachev's *glasnost* separatist policies, which reduced trade-preferences with the Soviet-bloc countries. More devastating, Gorbachev cut armaments production by well over 50%, with resulting unemployment, still minimal under the subsidized Communist system, but a source of unrest. The stagnant economy, unresponsive to his adjustments, created ever-longer queues for food and consumer items during his entire regime. Finally, *glasnost*, immediately endowing civil liberties, diminished the element of fear motivating Russia's entire system. His Nobel Peace Prize in 1990 was deservedly won for Peace, not Economics. On the sympathy side, consider the revelations facing the embattled reformer, hoping to achieve results from the top, rather than at the roots:

> ...I did not realize the true scale of the militarization of the country until I became general secretary. It turned out that military expenditure was not 16 per cent of the state budget, as we had been told, but rather 40 per cent, and 20 per cent, not 6 per cent, of gross domestic product.[5]

For the record, we can examine two key Gorbachev economic proposals. The first, in 1984, was made just prior to his becoming general secretary. The second, prepared for the annual Party plenum, or convocation, in the summer of 1987, occurred when Gorbachev's domestic good-will was still strong, but waning, and trouble for his administration was in the air. It was a few months before his initial showdown with Yeltsin over the pace of economic reform.

On December 10, 1984, a week before his inspired trip to visit Prime Minister Thatcher helped make him a world-figure and the leading candidate to replace Chernenko as general secretary, Gorbachev made a highly-revealing speech. It was addressed to a conference on ideological research in Moscow, the conference itself contradictory in a state supposedly at the end of ideology. Gorbachev enthusiasts like Archie Brown remind us that this was still the era of Brezhnev's heavy-handed "stagnation." Brezhnev had ruled for eighteen years (1964–1982). There followed a brief interlude of three years before the successive deaths of Andropov and Chernenko led the Politboro to choose the youthful, energetic candidate. The point is

Brezhnev had deliberately suppressed any regard for his predecessor Khrushchev, whose epic condemnation of Stalin in 1956 had stunned the world, resulting in Khrushchev's forced retirement as a non-person two years after the Cuban missile crisis. It was not a time to weigh the deficiencies of socialism or to question the validity of the Soviet empire.

Gorbachev, who had spent a good deal of his adult life under the glare of Brezhnev, skillfully introduced the ideas that would distinguish his own career. The speech was scarcely noted in the West, and only cursorily reported in *Pravda*, so that now it is only a museum-piece related to Gorbachev's ideological development. It spoke about the need for economic reform if the Soviet Union were to continue as a superpower against the US, and used the term *perestroika*, or restructuring, as the way to get there. It revealed the Gorbachev preference for "acceleration", not a big bang, to accomplish *perestroika*. It introduced elements of competition, democratization, and *glasnost*. Quite clearly, the objective was to embrace new thinking and institutional reform, directed toward better management and a technological catch-up for the economy, all within the reformable system.

* * *

On to 1987. By now Gorbachev's peace overtures and international approval for *perestroika* and *glasnost* have drawn attention away from the continuing decline and disorder in the economy, although the eventual impoverishment of 25% of the Russian population will appear years later on Yeltsin's doorstep. This was a heady period for Gorbachev. He has invited Andrei Sakharov, the conscience of the nation, and his wife, Yelena Bonner, to return to Moscow after six years of Brezhnev-imposed exile. *Perestroika* may not have made a dent in the economy, but his new book, *Perestroika: New Thinking for Our Country and the World* (1987), will sell five million copies in 160 countries and 80 languages, netting the author $3 million in royalties, all dutifully turned over to charitable purposes.[6] There are more trips abroad, India, China, and Italy, with a visit to the Pope. There are summits with Reagan, who visits Gorbachev in Russia in May 1988.

Thatcher visits Russia in 1987. In December 1988, "Gorby-mania" takes over New York when he addresses the United Nations, pledges troop reductions of 500,000, and renounces the use of force. Yet for three months in early 1987, this political phenomenon of the Cold-War period works continually on "the correct strategy" for a new try on economic reform, and finds himself completely frustrated by Party and bureaucratic opposition.

Rather than examine the dreary 40-page paper in detail, since it is now only an abandoned footnote in Russia's economic transition, a brief summary will indicate Gorbachev's position in his Politboro-approved recommendation to the Committee. The new model of his economic enterprise would be a "socialist producer," with "complete independence." The old concept of planning by decree would gradually become planning by recommendation and forecasting. The reforms would also embody a new type of price-determination which would combine market-mechanisms with state regulation. The rest involves detailed instructions for restructuring management procedures. A general statement asks Party committees to stay out of economic oper-ations and concentrate on ideology and other good endeavors.

We can now turn to Gorbachev's evaluation of his defeat:

> ...simple explanation: no one wanted to let go of power. The system needed shortages, otherwise the monopoly, along with its fellow-travellers – bribes, graft, mutual favors and so forth – would simply collapse... Resistance to radical economic reform would not abate and [even] the decisions we adopted would be torpedoed.[7]

What radical reforms? From Gorbachev's point of view, "radical" meant how deeply his management and efficiency reforms would go. Everyone was in favor of reform, he noted, but not on his own turf. The main opposition came from the major economic agencies of the state, Gosplan (State Planning Committee), Gossnab (State Commit-tee for Material and Technical Supply), and Minfin (Ministry of Finance), who, he claims, joined ranks with the conservative Party bosses to defeat the administration hands down.

More interesting is how far Gorbachev would diminish his loyalty to socialism at this mid-point of his regime. He refers with disdain to

97

the "command economy" as much as any free-enterpriser would, but he clearly believes he can combine elements of the market-system with socialism. He relates a clash of opinions at a long April 1987 work-session on the plenum paper with Ryzhkov, his personally-selected prime minister. Ryzhkov: "I cannot go beyond the framework of socialism." Gorbachev: "We will carry out reforms within the framework of socialism, but not within the framework that puts chains on society and extinguishes initiative and incentive."[8]

According to Gorbachev, Yeltsin sat through the 1987 Politboro preparation-sessions with little to say about the draft, except that Gorbachev should require more help from the Party, but Gorbachev on Yeltsin is suspect.[9] As usual, Yeltsin has the final, sharper word. In an interview with *Newsweek*, in 1992, he stated:

> He wanted to combine things that cannot be combined – to marry a hedgehog and a grass snake – communism and a market economy, public-property ownership and private-property ownership, the multi-party system and the Communist Party with its monopoly on power. But these things are incompatible.[10]

Gorbachev's Advisors

Gorbachev was interested in new thinking, the subtitle of his book *Perestroika*, the 1987 best-seller whose world-acclaim confirmed his self-perception in that respect. He enjoyed travelling outside the Soviet Union to share fresh thoughts, whether tilting with Margaret Thatcher or basking in the company of two intellectual favorites, Willy Brandt, the former German Chancellor, and Felipe Gonzalez, the prime minister of Spain. These statesmen, he believed, were living examples that forceful politicians could bring their countries from authoritarian rule into personal freedom and political tolerance. Moreover, they could dip into market-economy waters – far deeper than he would – and still find themselves socialists. Gonzalez was a particular favorite, in something like a father-son relationship. Gorbachev relates in his *Memoirs* how Gonzalez phoned Bush after the coup, seeking world support for the rescue of Gorbachev, which, of course was a lost cause once the dénouement of the inept fall was analyzed.[11]

Two of his closest advisors hold special interest. The first, Aleksandr Yakovlev, economist, diplomat, media expert, and liberal mentor from the beginning until he resigned in July 1991, frustrated at Gorbachev's turn to the right and inability to discern his friends from his enemies. The second, Eduard Shevardnadze, the handsome, white-haired, august Party chief from the Republic of Georgia, who was hand-picked by Gorbachev as foreign affairs minister to succeed the veteran opponent of the West, Andrei Gromyko. He, too, jumped ship in December 1990, later to return to Georgia to become its head of state, knowing it would secede from the Russian Federation, but in fact equally disillusioned with Gorbachev's domestic political and economic obtuseness. These two men, along with the loose-cannon Yeltsin, were the only true believers in economic reform, supporting the faint-hearted Gorbachev, in the Politboro. Yakovlev and Shevardnadze were uncannily prescient about the sinking of Gorbachev's regime.[12] They give us insight into two of his economic touchstones, the depth of his commitment to socialism and the limitations of his commitment to economic reform.

Yakovlev was a many-sided, urbane figure. A badly-wounded lieutenant in the marines at age eighteen, he abandoned plans to become a schoolteacher when the local Party officials for his village recruited him as a political trainee, their ranks sorely depleted by the ongoing war. He graduated from the Higher Party School in Moscow and moved on to the Moscow Central Committee headquarters. As the youngest instructor there, seated in the highest balcony, he heard Khrushchev's secret 1956 speech denouncing Stalin's purges and the murders of his Party and military colleagues. From that point on, Yakovlev was covertly dedicated to the idea of democracy, but equally intent on pursuing his career. With an advanced degree in history and philosophy, and currently head of the Central Committee's Department of Science and Culture, he was considered reliable and important enough to send to Columbia University in New York for a year of study. He wrote his thesis on the New Deal, useful for his later service as an architect of Gorbachev's *perestroika* program. Back in Moscow, he became a propaganda chief for press and television. Again his training was made to order for Gorbachev, for whom he would later become media director as well as image-handler. Gorbachev was a natural on TV, frequently appearing on the evening news, going over the heads of his opposition and enjoying saturation-coverage on government stations.

Sooner or later, Yakovlev's ambivalence would be noticed at headquarters. Perhaps for a writer's challenge, he interrupted his Party-line hack-work with a magazine article implicitly defending "intellectualism" as only a bare threat to Russia's "national spirit." Sensing the negative reaction, he allowed himself to be spirited away to Canada as Soviet Ambassador, where he spent ten happy years in exile, travelling, observing, and reading in a variety of disciplines. Even in that period, he authored, perhaps by habit as well as conviction, a standard book on America's doomed civilization.

In May 1983, the peripatetic Gorbachev, now a rising Politboro member, travelled to Canada, where he forged a strong bond with the forgotten ambassador. They explored each other's minds while flying over Canada, and agreed that Russia was at a critical crossroads, desperate for new leadership and ideas. Upon returning, Gorbachev managed to recall Yakovlev, place him in an appropriate think-tank, and then advance him head-over-heels to the Politboro after becoming general secretary. Most observers of the Gorbachev period credit Yakovlev with consistently backing and promoting every progressive policy initiated by Gorbachev, whether a matter of *perestroika* or *glasnost*. Unlike his associates at the Politboro, he was purely cerebral, having never run a ministry, an industrial plant, or a political region. In this respect, he was Gorbachev's brain-truster.

The Nina Andreyevna Affair

Yakovlev's steady hand is demonstrated in his response to a major media-attack on *perestroika* in 1988, during the "Prague Spring" of Gorbachev's administration, when his public popularity was still in the ascendant. The conservative opposition, unimpressed by Gorbachev's world-esteem and skillful use of the media, launched its own counterattack in what came to be known as the "Nina

Andreyevna Affair." Yegor Ligachev, Secretary of the Party Committee, became a full member of the Politboro (1985–1990), and was assigned to ideology, in which position he openly led the opposition to Gorbachev's programs. Early in 1988, Ligachev received a copy of a scorching indictment of Gorbachev's political and economic reforms sent to *Sovetskaya Rossiya*, a newspaper representing the most conservative wing of the Party. He secretly instigated the editors to embellish it and give it prominent treatment. The editors enthusiastically prepared the piece for the Sunday, March 13 issue, while Gorbachev was on his way to Yugoslavia, and Yakovlev to Mongolia. The full-page article, entitled by the author, Nina Andreyevna, "I Cannot Forsake Principles," was a passionate contradiction of everything Gorbachev, Yakovlev, and the liberal intelligentsia had been preaching for two years. Stop the talk about Stalin's mistakes, it urged, and give him credit for building the country and defeating the Nazis. The Gorbachev liberals are deviating from the accepted principles of socialist realism, creating nothing but ideological confusion in politics and the economy. It included standard anti-Semitism, a plea for the old moral values, and went beyond the terms of civil debate by calling for an immediate counter-revolution of action. Ligachev summoned a meeting of the leading editors and broadcast agencies, endorsing the "wonderful document." He notified the Tass news agency to recommend it to newspapers throughout the Union, and suggest they reprint it. Assuming the instructions were official, all but a few complied. Meanwhile, the conservatives in the Party issued underground pamphlets warning against "economic disaster and social upheaval leading to the country's enslavement by imperial states." In the next few weeks, while liberal editors speculated about a knock on their doors, Yakovlev took charge, fully aware that the anti-*perestroika* manifesto must have been sanctioned by the opposition leadership. He counselled caution and drafted an article for Gorbachev to run in *Pravda* on April 5, the gist of which follows:

> ...The cult [of Stalin] was not inevitable. It is alien to the nature of socialism and only became possible because of deviations from fundamental socialist principles ...The *Sovetskaya Rossiya* article is dominated by an essentially fatalistic perception of history...

Apparently wrapping Gorbachev's response in the mantle of true socialism carried the day. It is difficult to conceive that such shallow blows and turgid counterblows could agitate a nation of highly-literate readers, dedicated to poetry and the Russian novels. Yet how many of us have experienced a lifetime of forced education in such theology, including Yakovlev, superbly trained at state expense for his abandoned calling? The use of double-speak was of course commonplace in Soviet power circles. Scholars like Archie Brown, versed in the text, accordingly dissect at length Gorbachev's 1984 seminal speech, in which the cautious candidate moves substantially to the left by referring to "developing socialism" rather than "developed socialism" as the preferred state of the union.[13] At any rate, Gorbachev and Yakovlev managed to drop the subject rather than create further dissent within the Politboro. The liberal editors were reassured, and Ligachev's protestations of innocence were accepted.[14]

Turning to Gorbachev's version of the affair, he acknowledges some input from Yakovlev in his reply. He actually sees some merit in the contretemps, recording satisfaction that such a letter would not have been possible without his policies of *perestroika* and *glasnost.* Further, if there was so much nostalgia at large for the old order, it inspired him to lead the forthcoming 1988 All-Union Party Conference to enact further reforms. Most important he would secure passage of legislation by which the all-important semi-annual Party Conference delegates would be elected by Party members, not appointed. As a result, he states, the All-Union Conference readily approved what in retrospect seem to be more ineffective platitudes, "implementation of radical economic reform, activation of the spiritual potential of society, reform of the political system, and democratization of international relations." He notes that the ousted Yeltsin, attending as Moscow Party chief, went along with his recommendations.[15]

* * *

The foreign minister responsible for the democratization of international relations was Eduard Shevardnadze, a reassuring face to the relieved world as he negotiated the details of unexpected summits and treaties, mainly with America's Secretary of State, George P. Schultz, appearing on press and television as a civilized anodyne to the shoe-banging Khrushchev, the Molotov of Hitler's non-aggression pact, and the stolid Gromyko. What relationship did foreign policy have to do with economic reform? First, Shevardnadze functioned as liberal prod, testing Gorbachev to recognize reform experiments and devolution of the former Union republics, such as he had championed for his native Georgia. Second, there was the recognition by both men that there could be no effective economic reform while the Soviet Union persisted in its lop-sided defense expenditures, starting with a two-million army, that created not only a military-industrial complex of political opposition, but also seriously contributed to the mounting consumer shortages affecting the patience of the nation. This obstacle applied as well to the costs of occupying the Baltic states, Gorbachev's Chechnya, which Shevardnadze opposed.

A film episode highlights the influence of the few liberals like Shevardnadze in the Politboro and the increasing power of the mass media in Russian politics. Hedrick Smith, in Russia to produce a series of documentary programs for American television, *Inside Gorbachev's USSR*, was particularly sensitive to this aspect of *glasnost*. At the time, in spite of other shortages, TV sets were plentiful, attracting national audiences of 150 million, and movies, such as they were, could draw audiences of eighty million. A certain Tengis Abuladze had produced in Soviet Georgia a powerful film on the Stalinist terror, in the early 1980s. Shevardnadze told Smith that Brezhnev's Moscow censors had rejected the proposal for distribution in the Russian language. Shevardnadze had read the script several times and decided to allow its production in the Georgian language for Georgian television, exercising his power as Party chief. After production was completed in 1984, Shevardnadze had second thoughts, and decided it was too risky to release. When he was summoned by Gorbachev to become foreign secretary, he asked Gorbachev to let him fulfill his promise to the filmmaker. Gorbachev saw the film, gave his approval, and *Repentance*, in the Georgian language with Russian voice-overs, was soon shown throughout Russia. Tens of millions saw the film.[16]

Gorbachev's Attraction to Socialism

With the media at his command and the world applauding his international policies, Gorbachev was unable to break the logjam of the unproductive, inefficient economy, caught in the contradictory amalgam of command and *perestroika* systems, aggravated by the disintegration of the Soviet bloc, (the result of his own *glasnost*), and the shock of immense reductions in defense expenditure. It was not just the greed and power-preservation of the Party and bureaucrats that were sabotaging his efforts, as he complained in the wake of the 1987 Party Conference. His own unyielding devotion to the socialist economic model was equally at fault, leading to patchwork reforms intended to modernize socialism with initiative and incentive. Whatever the theoretical possibilities of this hybrid, it did not work for Gorbachev before his time ran out.

If further evidence is needed to prove Gorbachev's one-track obsession with the economic aspect of socialism, some quotes are available, bearing in mind that thinking-men like Gorbachev modify their ideas over time, and that none of us wants to be categorized by statements that may be out of context.

We have noted Gorbachev's own definition in his *Memoirs* about how much he could bend, in his 1987 conversation with his even more pious Prime Minister Ryzhkov, a high-type, thoroughly-experienced and competent bureaucrat, who finally left the scene with a massive heart attack, under the strain of events, in 1991. Next, we can hear from Gorbachev in an unusual television interview in December 1990, reported by the always reliable David Remnick. On the spur of the moment, stung by the increasing disapproval of Yakovlev and Shevardnadze, he revealed publicly for the first time that both his grandparents had been summarily imprisoned under Stalinism. He continued:

> I've been told more than once it is time to stop swearing allegiance to socialism... Why should I? Socialism is my deep conviction, and I will promote it as long as I can talk and work... Am I supposed to turn my back on my grandfather who was committed to the [socialist] idea?... When cleansing myself of Stalinism and all the other filth, would I

renounce my grandfather and my father and all they did?[17]

At this late point in his regime, Gorbachev's emotional commitment to socialism, and corresponding ingrained fear of private property, prevailed in relation to agriculture as well as industry. Food shortages had become serious, and foreign airlifts were being received. On 3 December, 1990, Yeltsin's maverick Russian republic passed its own law allowing farmers to buy land from the state, providing any resale would have to be back to the state. This would allow family farms to work side by side with collective farms, Yeltsin claimed, bearing in mind that the tiny *dachas* already produced – and still do – as much as a quarter of Russian food. Even this was too much for Gorbachev, fully aware that Deng Xiaoping had successfully privatized small-scale farms for more than a decade in China. In a Kremlin speech on 27 November, 1990, he said:

> Although in favor of the market, I do not accept private ownership of land... Should I renounce my grandfather, who was a collective-farm chairman for seventeen years? I cannot go against my father. Should I reject whole generations? Did they live in vain?[18]

Initiative and Incentive

Having pilloried Gorbachev as an unregenerate socialist, although dedicated to improving socialism, it is with some gratification that we identify him as a first-line contributor to the private enterprise-system after all. This is in relation to his sponsorship of the February 1988 legislation permitting cooperatives to act as legal enterprises. Cosmeticized under the title "cooperative," with its socialist over-tones, a Pandora's box was opened that slowly but surely swept though Russia. By Yeltsin's year 1995, official statistics report over 795,000 new small businesses had started from 1988 on, mainly under the cloak of this facade, and aside from the state-owned small-service firms turned over to their managers in Yeltsin's privatization process. At first, the Gorbachev legislation limited enterprises to three members of the firm, but the cap was quickly lifted.

What led Gorbachev to sponsor this heresy? The legislation is barely mentioned in his *Memoirs*, but he does write he admonished his surprised Finance Minister at the time: "Are we going to stifle the people's initiative as in the past, or shall we let them live and work? Don't be afraid that someone might get rich by his own hard work!"[19] This is a far cry from Deng's "Let everyone be rich!" but still a step on that road.

It is dangerous to speculate about what is in another's mind, but "initiative and incentive" may be the key. Gorbachev was a management pragmatist as well as economic idealist. His concept of industry in his immense country centered on the great socialized dams and pipelines, engineering combines, steel factories, and coal mines that symbolized Russia's war-victory and fostered its traditional production heroes. At the beginning of 1988, enterprises with more than 200 employees dominated the economy, accounting for about 95% of both employees and production, and 75% of these were in enterprises with more than 1,000 employees.[20] The farms, which he knew well from his pre-Moscow career, had to remain collective. The farmers preferred the values of that system, and any major changes, other than long-term leasing, of which he approved, would confront the fundamental property issue. Permitting individuals to engage privately in service, repair, and similar small enterprises, however, would demonstrate the benefits of initiative and incentive, sorely missing in Russian management. Even so, he notes in his *Memoirs*, the forces of reaction would thwart such endeavors, reflecting their rabid distrust of private enterprise at any level, and exercising their weapons of restrictive licensing and punitive taxation.[21]

The enterprises persisted, getting a headstart from the great network of underground and black-market activity that flourishes in any command economy. The reform economist Nicholas Schmelyov has estimated over ten million were engaged in such enterprise, a large proportion moonlighting on their state employment, refuting the theory that Russians by nature are not candidates for a market-system.[22] The big cities, like Moscow and the newly renamed St. Petersburg, their booster-mayors determined to make their cities showpieces of the new Russia, eased restrictions and cultivated the entrepreneurs. Soon their problems would be as much with shakedown-Mafias as with public authorities. A newspaper, *Kommersant*, promoted enterprise, and a nationwide trade association, led by a respected member of the Congress of People's Deputies, became an effective voice.

The ideologues did not give up easily on this bourgeois eruption. In late 1989, the Supreme Soviet moved to kill the entire cooperative movement, and only special pleading from Gorbachev's Deputy Prime Minister Abalkin, appearing on his behalf, saved the day. In 1990, the trade association scored two victories in court, a momentous innovation, against regional governments that had illegally shut them down *en masse* or sequestered their assets. The rule of law, without which a market-economy is helpless, was at least set in motion. Yakovlev, although more interested in market-reform than in socialist-reform, was enthused. "The future of the Soviet economy," he stated in 1989, "lies in cooperative socialism," putting an improbable spin on Gorbachev's vision.[23]

So much for Gorbachev's entrepreneurs, which he surely would not claim as a central accomplishment of his administration. The point is that a million new entrepreneurs, and their families and friends, constitute a formidable political influence in Russia, as in advanced capitalist countries, where such people provide over half of new jobs, especially in the rising service industries. If Russia succeeds in producing a viable market-system, it will be in no small part due to the political ideology as well as the economic accomplishments of this constituency.

Gorbachev and Yeltsin

It is tempting, although premature, to compare Gorbachev and Yeltsin. We certainly cannot look to either for a fair appraisal of the other, personally or in regard to program. Each represents his own segment of the transition period, with about equal time in power. Gorbachev had the more important inaugural, earth-shaking role. He ended the Cold War and let the Soviet bloc countries secede, permitting only minor bloodshed in the Baltic states. He failed in his attempt to preserve the rest of the Union, even the adjoining Russian Federation

107

states. He also failed in his attempt to reform socialism as an economic system in his allotted time. Yeltsin inherited the long-sought successor role, finally brought his way by an unexpected turn of events. He ended Gorbachev's dysfunctional, hybrid-economy by decisive action, with painful results over too long a time. Still he brought Russia across the line to a potential market-economy, compatible with democracy, but not an advertisement for capitalist-democracy in its present state. His Chechnya expedition was a gratuitous failure. It took both men to eradicate the aged, powerful Communist Party, but it is typical of their statesmanship that there were no purges or indictments by association. In fact it is remarkable that of the five coup leaders, two committed suicide, and the others are walking free. The Party endures as the largest vote-getter in the 1996 primary election. Like capitalism, it is being democratically tested in the marketplace.

On more trivial grounds, preferences can be expressed. Gorbachev admirers are turned off by his turn to the right in 1990, and his blind trust in the hardliners who betrayed him. His *Memoirs* contain a good deal of blame-assignment and lack of coherent discipline. His unfathomable decision to run for president in the 1996 elections, gaining less than one per cent of the vote, diminished his stature as an elder statesman.

Opinion-makers have varied estimates. The icon Solzhenitsyn went back to Russia and deplored Gorbachev's walking in place. He cannot stand Yeltsin's "predatory capitalism," but his own concept of Russian exceptionalism, in a spiritual garb, is not helpful. A cultural authority like Tatyana Tolstaya ends on the side of Gorbachev, finding Yeltsin too crude and conniving for her taste.[24] My own preference for persona, not accomplishment, is for the straightforward, large-hearted, tolerant Yeltsin, selecting a talented mix of associates, and relating to the people in the tradition of FDR and Truman. Whatever the outcome, the world is in debt to Gorbachev, and Russia, if it succeeds, will be in debt to Yeltsin.

Notes

1 Archie Brown, *The Gorbachev Factor* (New York: Oxford University Press), 317–18.

2 Boris Yeltsin, *Against the Grain: An Autobiography* (London: Jonathan Cape, 1990), 113–19.

3 Non-Marxist definitions of socialism challenge democratic capitalism to reform its house. They need not to be disconcerting as they generally avoid any connection with totalitarianism, either for state or economy. A good example is provided by Stuart Hampshire, the eminent British moral philosopher, who is also grounded in the political world. For Hampshire, no utopian theory but instead a set of moral injunctions and priorities for a democratically-elected government: reduction of poverty second only to defense; reduction of wealth-inequality to counter power-inequality; basic human needs to be delivered by the economy, even at the expense of more gross domestic product. (Letter to author of 10 September, 1995). The lifetime oeurvre of Robert Heilbroner is America's most eloquent and compelling examination of the nature and consequences of capitalism versus socialism.

4 Anders Åslund, *How Russia Became a Market Economy*, 34.

5 Mikhail Gorbachev, *Memoirs* (New York: Doubleday, 1995), 215.

6 Gorbachev, *Memoirs*, 238.

7 Gorbachev, *Memoirs*, 230–31.

8 Gorbachev, *Memoirs*, 227.

9 Gorbachev, *Memoirs*, 229.

10 *Newsweek*, 6 January 1992, 11–12.

11 Gorbachev, *Memoirs*, 662–63.

12 See Eduard Shevardnadze, *The Future Belongs to Freedom* (New York: Free Press, 1991), 210. "Gorbachev himself had been spoon-feeding the junta with his indecisiveness, his inclination to back and fill...his poor judgment of people...his distrust of the democratic forces, the very same people who had changed thanks to the *perestroika* he had begun. That is the enormous tragedy of Mikhail Gorbachev, and no matter how much I empathize with him, I cannot help but say it almost led to a national tragedy." Yakovlev was equally disillusioned. David Remnick, after the coup, received Yakovlev's most intimate recollections. In July 1991, Yakovlev told Remnick, when he left Gorbachev's staff before the coup, he pressed Gorbachev: "The people around you are rotten. Please, finally, understand this." "You exaggerate," Gorbachev replied. (Remnick,

Lenin's Tomb, 447).

13 Brown, *The Gorbachev Factor*, 79.

14 Remnick, *Lenin's Tomb*, 85; Gorbachev, *Memoirs*, 253.

15 Gorbachev, *Memoirs*, 256–57.

16 Hedrick Smith, *The New Russians* (New York: Avon Books, 1991 edition), 110–11.

17 Remnick, *Lenin's Tomb*, 149–50.

18 FBIS (Foreign Broadcast Information Service), 5 December 1990, reported in Smith, *The New Russians*, 232.

19 Gorbachev, *Memoirs*, 225.

20 Blasi, Kroumova, Kruse, *Kremlin Capitalism*, 25.

21 Gorbachev, *Memoirs*, 225, 228.

22 Nicolai Schmelyov and Vladimir Popov, *The Turning Point: Revitalizing the Soviet Economy* (New York: Doubleday, 1989), 199.

23 Smith, *The New Russians*, 291.

24 Tatyana Tolstoya, "The Way They Live Now," *New York Review of Books*, 4 April 1997, 13–15.

7 Václav Havel: A Principled Dissident

The Playwright Meets Power

When US Secretary of State Madeline Albright visited the Czech Republic in July 1997, she first repaired her lapsed awareness of her Jewish ancestry by visiting the Prague Jewish Cemetery and the synagogue bearing her grandparents' names on the Holocaust death-list. She then received the nation's highest reward from Václav Havel, president of the republic.

The two Czech figures made a memorable pair, the brilliant refugee who rose to become a high-level stateswoman in the citadel of democracy, and the legendary president who led the passive resistance that helped end forty years of Soviet occupation.

It is likely that Havel presented Albright with a personal gift of a bound copy of his selected speeches. Paul Wilson, Havel's translator into English, tells of this artifact, prepared for such occasions, in his preface to Havel's latest book, *The Art of the Impossible: Politics and Morality in Practise* (1997). Treasuring his own copy, Wilson notes that it is an unadorned, single-spaced, typed manuscript, reflecting the playwright-author's reverence for the written word. There is no room for speech-writers on Havel's staff.

Few authors have been served by such an exemplary translator. Wilson lived in Czechoslovakia from 1967 to 1977. Since his return to Canada in 1978, he has translated practically all of Havel's writings that have appeared in English. His lucid, compact translations are eloquent, so much so that he performs as Havel's official alter ego. A translator need not be a hero to his author, much less an objective authority, but Wilson qualifies as a point of reference.

In his preface to this latest book, he states the key to Havel's philosophy, however persuasive otherwise, is that his words are spoken from the heart. More specifically, from the heart as Havel's conscience. The conscience as moral arbiter has a long lineage. Adam Smith's reliance on the conscience as mirror of the heart is expressed repeatedly in his *The Theory of Moral Sentiments*, (1759). Smith is deliberately mentioned because an unexpected correspondence between Smith and Havel can be found in Havel's eventual endorsement of the market-system, to be discussed ahead.

With the heart as instigator, Wilson continues, the weapon is truth. Havel's mission has been to combat evil, whether the iron-boot of a dictator, or the more subtle brain-wash of Communist ideology, with the truth above all. "The truth shall make you free" is another venerable prescription, but as with all special observers, Havel makes us see the Soviet web of control, from his own experience, in sharper focus.

* * *

A place for encountering Havel in his early role as dissident is found in his 1978 essay, *The Power of the Powerless*. The title reflects his existence in an occupied country, whose people have become acquiescent and benumbed, seduced by token freedoms and benevolent ideology, their energy expended in getting along. His concern is with the underlying human drama and its Faustian choices, good and evil, politics and conscience, hope and submission. The scenario, however, is not millennial. There is no call to arms. Typically, the metaphor for his message arises from his own experience, a sign in a greengrocer's window.

Some background will be helpful. The essay was written as the central piece for a *samizdat*, or underground book, entitled *On Freedom and Power*.[1] It was written in the period between the Charter of 1977, signed by over one-hundred intellectuals, from a wide variety of Czechoslovakian cultural and political life, and the subsequent jailing and persecution of many of its signatories, with Havel, imprisoned for three years from 1979, heading the inmates' list.

112

Charter 77 was by later standards innocuous, except to the authorities. It called primarily for a commitment to the rule of law and the restoration of civic virtue on the part of Party officials and citizens alike. The 1978 essays differ in their proposed models for more freedom, but at that point, ten years before liberation, there was still the consensus, among the essayists, that some kind of socialism was salvageable, for example, the "socialism with a human face" of Dubcek's 1968 episode, repressed by Warsaw Pact tanks in the heart of Prague. Exposing the lies and hypocrisy of the system, whatever its name, was enough to gain imprisonment. More interesting, there is no call for capitalism or a market-system for the economy, either from Havel or his colleagues. The shared business at hand was essentially tactical. It called for a nationwide shadow-society, not with hidden guns, but with a parallel, innovative form of opposition.

It would be expressed in dynamic civic organizations, political discussion groups (in the one-party country), social societies, educational seminars, church groups, even fan-clubs for rock and roll addicts, apparently subversive beyond the comprehension of the authorities.[2] It was a vigorous attempt to awaken the silenced majority, beyond the hundred intellectuals, that might eventually become a political factor to be reckoned with. The restored civic society, meaning a society other than the all-pervasive state society, was not a quixotic idea. Such tactical opposition found a precedent in a mythic hero, Schweik the Good Soldier, the World War I infantryman who frustrated the militarists by playing dumb or compliant as the occasion demanded. On a loftier note, Franz Kafka had mortally wounded every state's bureaucracy by recounting his abject terror in front of their high desks. Havel idolized Kafka and proudly identified with Kafka's sense of guilt and alienation.[3] Finally, Havel and his compatriots were thoroughly aware of the Thoreau and Gandhi accomplishments in civil disobedience.[4]

The Power of the Powerless

Havel's 1978 essay opens with a reasoned analysis of why his country possesses faint hopes for liberation. He states Soviet

113

totalitarianism differs from "classical" totalitarianism, the apocalyptic, short-term rise and fall of Hitler, and Stalin's reign of terror, each associated with one man's monstrous career. So much so, that for analytical reasons, it requires a new name, post-totalitarianism. The conditions for its unique success start with the Cold-War period of stand-off between the world's remaining superpowers. Each is frozen in place by the other's nuclear capability. The Western superpower is ready with sympathy, but little else, for the benighted satellite countries. This imperviousness to outside threats has given the Soviet regime an unparalleled forty-year period to perfect its manipulative strategies for controlling a huge satellite population.

A second condition relates to the Soviet claim of roots in a benign social movement of long-standing tradition. This "undeniable historicity," although shamelessly perverted in practise by the Soviet dictatorship, derives its great authenticity from eighteenth and nineteenth-century proletarian and social movements. Its certainty about a "correct understanding" on how to resolve social and class conflicts, brought to a crescendo by Marx's creation of a strident, comprehensive political-economic system, is an existential fact, in force in half the world. "In its elaborateness and completeness," Havel notes, "it is almost a secularized religion." In the modern environment of eroded values and certainties, he adds, exercising his playwright's knowledge of human nature, "it has a certain hypnotic charm."[5] In other words, if you are going to exert dominion from distant Moscow, you are well-served by an eschatological, utopian ideology. Give power to the powerless.

A final condition is Havel's location of post-totalitarian power in state-ownership and direction of the means of production, nationalizing the entire economy itself, from housing to the giant Skoda works. In retrospect, the massive program of nationalizing every property instrument in the satellite countries, regardless of cost or consequence, defies understanding. It is not a requirement for authoritarian control, either in the fascist arrangement, or for the return of Hong Kong, a far-larger economy than any satellite, to China. The Soviet thoroughness is reminiscent of the fanatical record-keeping of the Nazis, seeking racial annihilation in the Holocaust, yet recording the minutest details of the obscene process. What kind of absolute devotion to theory impelled this cleansing-rage against private property, a hundred years after Marx, in advanced technological countries? We have noted its hold on such a large-minded man as Gorbachev in the previous chapter. At any rate, Havel acutely sensed its power. If you control a man's source of work and bread, and leaven it with cradle-to-grave benefits, regardless of lost freedoms, you are half-way home. The dissidents were faced with a Sysiphean task, using one of Havel's favorite adjectives.

* * *

From the view of our interest in Havel's growing attachment to the market-economy, the 1978 analysis is significant. He was forming an unqualified association of democracy with capitalism, or at least with capitalism's free-market component. Havel came from a wealthy family, his grandfather being a major architect and builder in Prague. When the Russians came in, the family properties were sequestered. Because of his father's ongoing usefulness, the family retained three rooms in their former mansion. Havel early exhibited dissidence, and was unable to gain admittance to higher education. He spent four years in a Technical High School as a lab technician, with evening courses in grammar. After two years in the army, he finally found employment as a stage-hand, and the rest is history. Add several prison-terms, including the depressing 1979–1982 period, for Havel's character-formation. He was offered exile to America in 1982, while sick in prison, but refused. Margaret Thatcher, also a lab technician before entering politics, recalls her excitement on reading Hayek and Friedman at that stage of her life.[6] Havel, self-educated, rejected the excesses of state regulation from first-hand experience.

The Sign in the Greengrocer's Window

Having analyzed the special nature of Soviet power, Havel makes a personal observation:

> The manager of a fruit and vegetable shop places in his window, among the onions and carrots, the slogan: "Workers of the world, unite!"

115

From this jolting setting, Havel unveils the awful reach of ideology, the artificial web needed to bind the populace at large to forced authority. It is the theatre of the absurd, but terrifying in its implications. Everyone knows the greengrocer, the humblest of traders, would prefer to concentrate on his onions and carrots, and that the placard no doubt was received with the wholesaler's shipment, and on and on to the summit of arbitrary power. The sign is obviously irrelevant to the produce, but perhaps by now the greengrocer endorses the message, announcing his affiliation with workers wherever they are as a good thing. Or is he, more likely, certifying his compliance as a member in good standing, hoping the authorities will let him conform and leave him alone? Whatever the motivation, Havel makes his point, the emperor has no clothes but force, and the powerless have allowed themselves to be enmeshed in a barrage of false ideology.

* * *

In 1986, three years before liberation, a *samizdat* book of questions and answers circulates among the dissidents. Havel has responded to fifty questions sent to him by a colleague in West Germany. They cannot visit each other, so taped questions and answers are exchanged, and the book prepared for the underground by Havel. The book was eventually reprinted by a Prague publisher within days after liberation, the first legal reprint of a *samizdat*.[7]

In it, Havel, the man of truth, is particularly candid and self-searching. The questions are often harsh. How do you explain your bourgeois origins? Isn't it time for the movement to renounce all traces of socialism? What about your reported attraction to Catholicism? Why are your *samizdat* prison letters to your wife, (*Letters to Olga*), so lacking in sentiment? Havel followers can pursue these aspects of this highly-honored, complex man. For our purposes, his answers about an economic system, at this point in his career, are noteworthy:

> The most important thing is that man should be the measure of all structures, including the economic... An economy that is nationalized and centralized has a catastrophic effect on all such [personal] relationships, which is why this type of economy works so badly... A worker's

activity is dissipated in the anonymous, automatic functioning of the system... All the natural forces of economic life, such as human inventiveness and enterprise, just payment for work done, market relations, competition, and so on, are scrapped.[8]

So much for the discredited command economy. Can a good word be put in for capitalism?

I don't believe all we need do...is bring back capitalism... It is well-known that enormous multinational corporations are curiously like socialist states, with industrialization, centralization, specialization, monopolization...IBM certainly works better than the Skoda plant, but both companies have long since lost their human dimension and have turned man into a little cog in their machinery... It is important, in short, that neither the superficial variety of capitalism, or the repulsive grayness of socialism, hide the deep emptiness of life devoid of meaning.[9]

Where can one find such participatory capitalism, embracing human, life-fulfilling objectives?

Given this, I would favor an economic system based on the maximum plurality of many decentralized, structurally-varied, and preferably small enterprises that respect the nature of different localities and traditions...a plurality of modes of ownership... Any central regulation of this variegated economic scene should be based on nothing but what contributes to the general good of the human being... The referee in such matters could not be a state bureaucracy but a democratically-elected political body that relies on a continuing dialogue between public opinion and expert opinion.[10]

In context, Havel's ideal capitalism seems hopelessly anachronistic, not practical, or pragmatically possible. None of the transition countries, including his own, are close to this moral vision, whatever the flaws of their present achievements. Criticism based on such excerpts should be modulated. Beware in general of public-definers of human goods and moral values, a skeptic like Isaiah Berlin might warn. What about capitalism's undeniable cornucopia of goods, available for more and more people? Take your choice of onions and

117

carrots, and rely on adequate regulations at the boundaries, available from the democratically-elected state.

Havel never claimed to be an economist. His economic goals, like his political goals, embrace "the art of the impossible." The eloquent vibrations of his total writings and moral leadership have made him a world-honored force. Criticism will hardly deter him from his rounds of responsibility, which he asserts life itself appoints to each of us.

* * *

In fairness, Havel's elliptic endorsement of the market-economy should be updated. The Havel of the 90s is no longer so concerned with the size and ambience of enterprise. He is consistently firm that the market-system is the only choice for a functioning democracy, especially in its role of creating a civic space that keeps the encroaching state at bay.

In this respect, the most thorough and considered recording of his economic-system beliefs are found in a 1992 book, *Summer Meditations*. He notes it was written during a short holiday amidst the break-up of his nation into the Czech and Slovak Republics, a time when he felt the need to clarify his opinions. The country had already embarked on shock-therapy reforms, involving the first wave of industrial privatization, a predictable source of criticism.

He wryly recalls that some have branded him "an exponent of the right" who wanted to bring capitalism back to the country, while others accuse him of harboring out-and-out socialist tendencies. Accustomed to such equal time, Havel rejects both labels and restates his self-perception as a matter of "temperament, a non-conformist state of the spirit, an anti-establishment orientation, an aversion to philistines, and an interest in the wretched and humiliated."[11]

Comfortable in this description, Havel states that although his heart may be left-of-centre, he has always known that:

> The only economic system that works is a market-economy, in which everything belongs to someone – which means that someone is responsible for everything...
> We have always stressed that we wanted a normal market-system of

economics. The program of breaking up the totalitarian system and renewing democracy would founder if it refused to destroy the basic pillar of that system, the source of its power and the cause of the material devastation it led to – that is, the centralized economy...[12]

The "disturber of the peace" is not willing to let free-marketers off without conditions. First, Havel claims that the marketplace and morality must not be mutually exclusive. The marketplace can work only if it has its own morality, enshrined in laws, regulations, and traditions – the rules of the game. Second, he charges that the public debate over the economy is uncovering right-wing dogmatism about markets that is as bothersome as left-wing prejudices, illusions, and utopias. Taking a side-shot at his prime minister, Václav Klaus, a doubt-free free-enterpriser, he states: "The cult of 'systematically pure' market economics can be as dangerous as Marxist ideology, because it comes from the same mental position...of theory."[13]

Klaus and his business-party have prevailed since 1991, largely because their program has worked. The Czech Republic, as noted in chapter 4, has successfully made the transition turn. Havel has long since become the honorary president, a hero of his country, but not the political leader. With Klaus's present troubles, largely arising from the inadequate financial regulation of unfettered capitalism, the moral advantage is once again with Havel.

Notes

1 "The Power of the Powerless" has appeared several times in English, notably in *The Power of the Powerless: Citizens Against the State in Central-Eastern Europe* (London: Hutchinson, 1985). The comments about the other essays are from Steven Lukes, who wrote the Introduction to the 1985 book, reprinted in Steven Lukes, *Moral Conflict and Politics* (London: Oxford Press, 1991), 257–75.

2 See Paul Berman, *A Tale of Two Utopias* (New York: W.W. Norton & Company, 1996), 195–253. Berman, a social critic, compares the utopias of the sixties with the rock and roll craze among the youth of the Czech underground period, wanting affiliation with the West, particularly America. There were, he states, a thousand such bands in Czechoslovakia before the

Prague Spring ended. Havel had spent six weeks in New York in 1968, participating in Joseph Papp's Shakespeare Festival, putting on his own play, *The Memorandum*, and returning to Czechoslovakia with prized rock-albums for his collection. When Berman visited Prague in the first weeks after the election, he had been preceded by rock-star Frank Zappa, who went immediately to the presidential palace for a photo-meeting with Havel.

3 Address at the Hebrew University, Jerusalem, 26 April 1990, in Václav Havel, *The Art of the Impossible, Politics and Morality in Practise* (New York: Alfred A. Knopf), 1997, 29–31.

4 Address at New Delhi, 8 February 1994, on receiving the Indira Gandhi Prize, Havel, *Art of the Impossible*, 152–61.

5 "The Power of the Powerless," in Václav Havel, *Open Letters* (New York: Vintage Books, 1992), 129.

6 Margaret Thatcher, *The Path to Power* (New York: Harper Collins, 1995), 50–51, 567.

7 Václav Havel, *Disturbing the Peace* (New York: Vintage Books, 1991), vii.

8 Havel, *Disturbing the Peace*, 13.

9 Havel, *Disturbing the Peace*, 14.

10 Havel, *Disturbing the Peace*, 16.

11 Václav Havel, *Summer Meditations* (New York: Vintage Books, 1993), 61.

12 Havel, *Summer Meditations*, 62.

13 Havel, *Summer Meditations*, 66. For a recent statement of the differences between Havel and Klaus, see "Rival Visions," *Journal of Democracy*, January 1996. In this article, excerpts from speeches and a television forum are juxtaposed and printed in the Warsaw daily *Gazeta Wyborcza*, 14–15 January 1995, edited by Adam Michnik (see next chapter). A commentary is provided by Petr Pithart, prime minister of Czechoslovakia before the break-up. Pithart scores each man for his rigidity: Havel for moralizing, and Klaus for disregarding the benefits of a civil society, which Klaus feels may be just another impediment to a self-correcting market society.

8 Adam Michnik: Choosing Liberalism

When Adam Michnik, Poland's leading intellectual dissident of the Cold-War period, arranged in 1995 to reprint the rival visions of Václav Havel and Václav Klaus for his newspaper *Wyborcza Gazeta*, Warsaw's leading journal, he was demonstrating his intense interest in the kind of political-economy that was emerging in the transition countries.[1] The velvet-revolutions were in the name of democracy and freedom, certainly not in the name of capitalism. Still, eight years later, the political transformation is assured, despite the return of Communist political figures to lead the administrations in all the major Central and East European countries, other than Russia and the Czech Republic. No country has reverted to the Soviet system, and most of the debate centers on the fortunes and perils of the market-system.

There are many similarities between Havel and Michnik. Both are men of considerable personal charm. They are upright personages, popular on all sides, regardless of differences within their countries. Each is associated in the public eye with a commitment to truth. They have high regard for each other. Michnik has gratefully acknowledged Havel's inspiration for their respective non-violent revolutions. Their collaboration goes back at least to 1978, with the Czech-Polish proposed *samizdat, On Freedom and Power,* in which Havel's *The Power of the Powerless* was the centrepiece essay. It turned out to be a Czech-only production, when the unexpected election of Lech Walesa as president of Poland in 1989 drew Michnik and others to Walesa's side in the task of forming a government and its policies.

Both men are born-writers, and freedom-fighters from childhood. The mental transformation for Michnik was more agonizing. Havel, as noted, came from an unreconstructed propertied family. Michnik, born in 1946, thirteen years Havel's junior, describes his parents as "Polish Communists of Jewish origin."[2] In pre-liberation Poland, his father had become enough of a supporter of his son's anti-Communist activities to join a hunger strike in a church in support of the release of Michnik and others from prison. During a later imprisonment, thirty Nobel Laureates petitioned General Jaruzelski for his release.

* * *

Eva Hoffman, in a widely-praised narrative, *Exit into History, A Journey through the New Eastern Europe* (1993), returned to her Polish homeland in 1991 and 1992 to witness first-hand the aftermath of liberation.[3] She comments on the ideological conflict between generations experienced by her friends, many in the Polish intellectual and literary worlds, reminding us of Western insulation from Cold-War cultural terrors, restricted to less painful variations associated with McCarthyism and peace demonstrations. A friend Helena, co-editor of Michnik's paper since its founding by Solidarity leaders at the start of Walesa's regime, recounts the excitement and dangers experienced before liberation by the non-violent dissidents, moving from apartment to apartment, blindly trusting in safe-havens, as they published their underground tracts and letters to the authorities. The movement consisted of an unusual alliance of workers, energized by Solidarity, which at its peak had over ten million members, and thousands of so-called intellectuals, inspired by a thirst for democracy, a high moral-orientation, infused by the predominant Catholic church and Pope John Paul II in one of their finest hours, and a toned-down patriotism, not narrow, but more aptly termed love of country. Helena's father was then the Communist Party's chief of propaganda, but the family discreetly kept to their own worlds. Another friend Marta, exemplifying Hoffman's discovery of an important feminist contribution, imprisoned in 1968, was offered a conditional release by the head of state, engineered by her grandfather and father, a prominent Communist. The three generations met in prison. The non-Communist grandfather set the terms: "We do not plead for mercy," he stated, to the relief of all. Pride, stubbornness, and patriotism

122

helped salvage their Polish psyche, badly bruised in world opinion by Poland's dark strain of intolerance.

* * *

This, then, is the world of Adam Michnik, of socialist heritage, a working editor and commentator on the same paper for close to a decade, moving in Havel's majestic orbit, but grounded in the daily world of editorials, advertising, and circulation. He runs what is technically a cooperative enterprise, with all the stock owned by the employees, but it is profit-dependent, in the sense that it is not subsidized, and must generate cash-flow for equipment replacement, contract negotiations, and to meet competition. Unlike Russia's embarrassing sales of media shares to banks and monopolists, Michnik's editorial support cannot be bought.

He has long since declared independence from Lech Walesa and the Solidarity party, and his masthead no longer bears the party logo. The parting must have been painful. Walesa is his son's godfather. Ostensibly the reason had to do with Walesa's turn to elements of national populism and intolerance. A further cause is said to be the former shipyard worker's dismay about the paper's comments on his educational limitations, leading to Walesa's unsuccessful demand for Michnik's resignation.[4]

* * *

The president of Poland is now Aleksandr Kwasniewski, who won a run-off election against Walesa in November 1995, and took office 23 December, 1995, age forty-one. He is the founder of the Democratic Left Alliance party, which was formerly the Communist party. The same sequence of Party-associated return to power has taken place in Hungary as well, while the Communist Zyuganov almost captured Russia in 1996. Some observations about Kwasniewski will update the march to capitalism in the transition countries.

Kwasniewski asserts he supports free markets, mass privatization, and integration with Europe. What kind of Communist is this? The answer, says the young President, is that ideology is no longer the

123

issue. Like the Czech Republic's Klaus, he feels pragmatism, what works and is fair, should be the deciding issue.

This is not a time for a return to the discredited Soviet command economy, he asserts, but neither is it the time for the absolute moral objectives and character transformation advocated by Havel. His administration, he blandly says, is a new-style Communist party favoring economic reform, political flexibility, and international trade. The advantage of redefining and renaming old parties comes to mind, applied by other young leaders, President Clinton and Prime Minister Tony Blair. The major continuity, of course, is Kwasniewski's confirmation of privatization, which we have noted is the defining, irreversible strategy for changing to a market-economy.

Doesn't this "shock-treatment" open the door to capitalist unemployment and corruption? Possibly, he answers, but in the long-run unemployment can only be remedied by economic growth, and there is plenty of room for that in Poland, starting with its low GDP and aided by tools of any label, namely, efficiency, competition, new enterprises, and exports on the part of its thirty-nine million population.

A devil's advocate might continue on the socialist side: Then what is worthwhile remaining of the Communist idea? Kwasniewski's answer is "social justice." We were elected by democratic vote not because of our similarity to Walesa's free-market program, but because enough people sensed there was still something terribly wrong in Poland. The state has a role to play. Older people want security, and younger people are ready to redefine social justice. They don't need egalitarianism from the economy, but they want equality of opportunity, through education, training, and nourishment in basic human needs, in order to become productive citizens.

Kwasniewski sees this choice as a world-situation. Through shared communications and technology, we know what is going on elsewhere and want our share of democracy and its prospects of economic well-being:

> Without the old ideological barriers, today we are very practical in taking the good things that work from many ideologies. Social democrats now accept many liberal concepts, especially in the economy... This new pragmatism is the reason I can easily relate to

Václav Klaus, Helmut Kohl, or Jacques Chirac – all from parties of the so-called "right." ...Now is the time of pragmatists.[5]

* * *

Michnik and Liberalism

Is there justification for this chapter's title, "Adam Michnik: Choosing Liberalism"? My objective is to defend capitalism, allied with liberalism, as the preferred system of choice wherever there is a choice. Michnik might wryly remind us that he did not spend three years in prison, in the prime of his life, to secure the market-system for Poland. His honorary degree from the New School of Social Research, his favorite sponsor of seminars at home and abroad, presented in Warsaw in 1984, was for human rights, not materialism. Michnik, by his own definition, is a "radical democrat," a reference to his politics rather than economics. A man of sharp humor, he might advise us to bestow the market-encomium on the English Adam Smith, the Austrian Hayek, or the American Friedman. Not that he is a hero to economists in his own country. Leszek Balcerowicz, noted in chapter 4 as the distinguished free-market disciple of such authorities, who coolly supervised Poland's successful shock-therapy program, overlooks Michnik's existence in his official history of his country's economic transition.

* * *

The Soros Conversion

As with Kwasniewski's odyssey, some unlikely role-reversals and re-identifications have arisen from the collapse of socialism and the triumph of capitalism. A disarming example would be George Soros, the billionaire financier who has made a mission of contributing money for market-reform purposes to his native Hungary, from which he fled in 1947, and over a dozen other former Communist countries.

125

Estimates vary, but the gifts amount to at least a munificent $1 billion, largely donated through Soros Foundations established in these and other countries.[6] The flow of money started in the earliest period of transition, when Western governments and international aid-agencies were locked in slow-motion. Soros's announced objective was to "transform the Soviet-bloc into thriving capitalist democracies," certainly a clear statement.

Anyone following the news items about Soros is aware of ongoing harassment, punitive taxation, and sequestering of funds in some of the donee countries (Belarus and Croatia, for example), apparently unwilling to tolerate such subversion. For our purposes, Soros has recently surprised supporters and critics by presenting his own revision. In a cover story for *The Atlantic Monthly* (February 1997), he asserts laissez-faire capitalism is too highly committed to the uninhibited pursuit of self-interest, and must be tempered by a recognition of a common-interest priority over particular interests. Otherwise, he warns, the whole capitalist system may break down. On balance, the article appears to advocate regulated capitalism, modified by an infusion of civic society of the type advocated by Havel and Michnik.[7] Billionaires are unpredictable, and Soros should be able to pontificate about capitalism without undue commotion. At any rate, he has not lost his commercial instinct. His new passion is an epic battle to win the privatization sweepstakes in Russia's sale of 25% of Svyazinvest, its telephone monopoly. The $1.88 billion winning-bid was from a group of Western and Russian banks allied with Soros's Quantum venture-fund, not all his own money this time. His opponents have asked Yeltsin to set aside the award.

A Brief History of Liberalism

We leave the self-confident, somewhat-tainted Soros. Can we establish a credible association on the part of the skeptical, philosophical Michnik with liberalism, the political foundation of capitalism, in the light of Michnik's transition experience? Can we authenticate his choice of liberalism as a fundamental priority?

The first requirement for this project is to set aside a definition of

126

liberalism, popular among skillful but highly-partisan media commentators. Participants are asked to check at the door any attribution of liberalism as the dreaded "L" word, a remnant from Cold-War politics, with unworthy antecedents from Senate-investigations onward. The power and threat of this definition, often preceded by "pointy-headed," cannot be denied, but its usefulness in sensible argument has terminated. When associated with New Deal tendencies to "tax and tax and spend and spend," it is factually true, but that bi-partisan depression-fix is over and done with. Conservatives have a much better claim against liberalism's generic tendency to overgovern domestic life, and to overregulate, and thus inhibit, economic growth, items which appear to be valid political-economic deductions world-wide.

Actually, liberalism has very respectable roots in the history of ideas. A risky, brief summary will suffice, first at its time of birth. The classical origins of modern liberalism, keeping in mind our interest in the market-society, would surely include John Locke, Adam Smith, and James Madison, theorists concerned with the right to economic liberty, notably the right to own private property and enjoy the fruits thereof, as an antidote to the arbitrary sovereign state. Any satellite-survivor like Michnik knows from first-hand experience that this concern was superseded by Soviet adherence to Marxist theory, which claims that such property was the source of an unfair, indeed conspiratorial, alliance between state and property-owners to retain power over the vast majority of citizens. This was not an entirely unworthy claim, considering the evidence, including modern slavery and labor-repression, and the fact that ownership of property has had only a brief post-feudal existence in the scheme of history. In practise, however, the Soviet choice was a deadly cure, especially in relation to the centuries-old primary concern of liberalism, to extract political freedom, or at least consent, from the arbitrary sovereign state.

Also, in the history of ideas, note should be taken of a series of intellectual contributions underlying the eventual triumph of liberal capitalism, preceding the anti-state inspiration. The leading historian in that area is Albert O. Hirschman, a distinguished analyst of pro-business, pro-trade sentiments in what might be termed capitalism's final gestation period, the late seventeenth century. He describes the

127

intense debate in that period over the passions and the interests. These archaic concepts, in common usage among opinion-makers such as Montesquieu, from France to the Dutch Republic, emphasized the benign effects of the interests, specifically trade and commerce, over the passions, referring to the religious and territorial wars plaguing the times.[8] By the nineteenth century, the so-called Manchester-liberals, England's party of traders and manufacturers, had created the modern political-economic relationship. On the theory side, Bentham's co-incident utilitarian moral philosophy, widely accepted, measured liberalism's success by its unemotional commitment to utility, a step away from compassion, but appealing to the individualist, yet phil-anthropic, men of property.

Again, over-simplified, liberalism's encounter with capitalism is illustrated in America's dynamic Progressive political movement of the pre-World War I period. Socialism, in America's non-European, non-revolutionary raiment, was still a seriously-proposed public choice, unsoiled by the eventual apostasy of the Soviet empire. By contrast, a midstream-majority of Americans preferred the Progress-ive program of a strong government, able to restrain capitalism in the face of its threatening disparities in power and benefits. This was the high-tide of American liberalism, with a full history of its own, beyond this study. For example, John Dewey, the country's leading philosopher and social critic, based in the liberal and pragmatic camps, rejected capitalism as beyond repair.[9] Other roots of liberal-ism, notably the Calvinist source of America's "agonized conscience," are amply recorded.[10]

Finally, the political theorists report there is a psychological premise for liberalism, namely the fragility of reason. Eighteenth-century rationalism, treated as if it were a live construct rather than an abstract theory, is said to lack heart, which liberalism's developing attachment to social justice, or at least to social amelioration, provides. In this respect, we can visualize Havel, Kwasniewski, and Michnik standing together on behalf of their national states, their hands left of center where the heart is, expressing deep concern for the disadvantaged, a current aspect of liberalism, good or muddled, as one wishes.

* * *

Letters to Michnik

In *Liberalism's Crooked Circle: Letters to Adam Michnik*, Ira Katznelson, professor of political science and history at Columbia University, challenges Michnik to come back from his abandoned socialism. In effect, he asks Michnik to broker a marriage between Katznelson's depiction of a disabled, ineffectual liberalism with socialism's still-redeemable dowry of social justice. Michnik's measured reply will help resolve this chapter's inquiry.

Katznelson is a veteran of scholarly conferences on democracy in Central Europe, held at home and abroad, co-chaired by Michnik, under the sponsorship of the New School for Social Research, where Katznelson formerly taught. Cast as an unusual literary device, unsolicited letters to Michnik, the book is basically a platform for Katznelson's eloquent and masterful history of liberalism's association with the political left, now reeling from the Soviet débacle. It is a reminder that a history of liberalism should also include views from both the left and the right of the liberal spectrum. This arrangement goes beyond the usual concerns of defenders of liberalism, content with judging liberalism as the designated center of the overarching spectrum of political democracy. The metaphor for the book's title comes from Michnik's underground Warsaw study group, The Club of the Crooked Circle. Not a thieves' seminar, but intellectuals dedicated to the rounding-off of liberalism's imperfect circle, in preparation for the end of the socialist occupation.

Katznelson's appeal reflects his high regard for Michnik as Central Europe's emblematic liberal-intellectual, by background a better prospect than Havel. We can understand Katznelson's search. Presenting a critical case for Western liberalism, he asserts it is "now at the mercy of libertarian, authoritarian populist, nakedly racist, and elitist versions," occupying the right wing of liberalism's spectrum. Additionally, like John Dewey and England's Harold Laski, he sees little redemptive capacity in capitalism, regulated or otherwise, although Katznelson asserts "the elimination of private property is neither possible nor desirable."[11]

In declining the offer, in an article entitled "Gray is Beautiful: Thoughts on Democracy in Central Europe," *Dissent*, Spring 1997,

Michnik rejects the extremes of the black of conservatism and the red of radicalism for his geographical domain. He first celebrates the multipluralist cultural eminence of the small, adjoining countries, typified in the works of Havel, Milan Kundera, Czeslaw Milosz, Eugene Ionesco, Georg Lukács and others. "This great cultural diversity...was the best defense against the claims of ethnic and ideological power." Now that the occupiers have left, he is more concerned about the reemergence of ethnic and religious conflicts than the fine-shadings of political or economic theory. He reminds us of the differences in the 60s, from which he emerged. "The students of Warsaw and Prague were fighting for the freedom that bourgeois democracy guaranteed...the students of Berkeley and Paris were fascinated by revolutionary rhetoric, of which the students of Warsaw had had enough." True, the common denominator was justice, but in retrospect, "there was something frightening in the West: vandalized universities, barbarian slogans that substituted for intellectual reflection, violence, terror, and political killings." Having chastened us for our children's hubris, he moves on to his own search for wisdom. "What remains of the idealistic-faith in the freedom-oriented socialism of the sixties?" he asked Jürgen Habermas, a distinguished European observer. "Radical democracy," Habermas answered, which Michnik accepts as his operating base. It is hardly an endorsement of socialism, but it implicitly demands more from democracy.

Michnik moves on to the alliance of parliamentary democracy with the problematical market-economy system. Communism was rejected for all the obvious reasons of lies, contradictions, and enslavement. "It also produced a grotesquely deficient economy, while we sought rationality, efficiency, and affluence." Michnik then makes a personal confession. By nature he is uncomfortable with all types of absolutism, reflected in his search for accommodation, not revenge, in regard to his former enemies, for which he has been frequently condemned. Absolute conviction about the enemy worked for Solzhenitsyn, Havel, and himself while under siege. In the world of post-conflict, however, where democratic procedures are being built on the rubble of totalitarian dictatorship, he prefers relativism, no more utopias, including economic egalitarianism. He is aware that free-market liberals will seek to place the economy first.[12] They can be met by opposing forces in a multi-pluralist setting, an evolving rather than final system. In effect, he is telling us to trust democracy. At any rate, there is no temptation to endorse Katznelson's hybrid-socialism at this time.[13]

Notes

1 See *supra*, Chapter 7, n. 13.

2 Introduction by Jonathan Schell, in Adam Michnik, *Letters from Prison* (Berkeley: University of California Press, 1985), xix.

3 Eva Hoffman, *Exit into History* (New York: Penguin Books, 1994), 1–119.

4 Adam Michnik, "My Vote Against Walesa," *New York Review of Books*, 20 December 1990. Eva Hoffman states she was interviewing Michnik in 1990 when Walesa's letter arrived demanding Michnik's resignation, which he forthwith refused. A year later she reports the intellectual rift. See Hoffman, *Exit into History*, 59, 65. See also "More Humility, Fewer Illusions – A Talk between Adam Michnik and Jürgen Habermas," *New York Review of Books*, 24 March 1994, for a more heated explanation: "...I was forced to read in the papers every day that I was a crypto-Communist. And this simply because I thought it would be wrong to hang General Jaruzelski... Solidarity supporters yielded to the temptation...of intellectual blackmail.", 28.

5 Aleksandr Kwasniewski, "MTV, NATO and Post-Communism in Poland," *New Perspectives Quarterly*, Spring 1996, 9–11.

6 See *New Yorker*, "The Pot Perflex, Mr. Soros's Agenda," 6 January, 1997, 4. The article refers to a recent *New York Times* article for the $1 billion figure. Also see Kevin F. Quigley, *For Democracy's Sake, Foundations and Democracy Assistance in Central Europe* (Baltimore: Johns Hopkins University Press, 1997), 87–102.

7 George Soros, "The Capitalist Threat," *Atlantic Monthly*, February 1997, 45–58. The article includes a claim that Soros "started supporting the Charter 77 movement in Czechoslovakia in 1980 and Solidarity in Poland in 1981." Assuming he did, neither movement would be happy with this publicity. They did not need outside money, and would reject implications of obligation.

8 Albert O. Hirschman, *The Passions and the Interests: Political Arguments for Capitalism before Its Triumph* (Princeton: Princeton University Press, 1977).

9 Alan Ryan, *John Dewey and the High-Tide of American Liberalism* (New York: W.W. Norton & Company, 1995), 30, 33, 310–11.

10 John Patrick Diggins, *Max Weber, Politics and the Spirit of Tragedy* (New York; Basic Books, 1996), 1–16, 92–109.

11 Ira Katznelson, *Liberalism's Crooked Circle, Letters to Adam Michnik*, (Princeton: Princeton University Press, 1996), 64–70. For a mainstream, rather than leftstream, critique of liberalism and its theory, see Stephen Holmes, *Passions and Restraints, on the Theory of Liberal Democracy* (Chicago: University of Chicago Press, 1995). Holmes, professor of political science at University of Chicago, emphasizes liberalism's balancing role between the psychological motivations, or passions, of individuals, and the institutional restraints of democratic institutions, such as constitutional law. From this confident stance, he does not share Katznelson's alarms about the survival of liberalism. See also Stephen Holmes, "Liberalism in the Ruins," *Foreign Affairs*, September/October 1997, 126–33. In this article, reviewing Katznelson's book, he in effect doubts whether the proposed marriage of liberalism with socialism will reach the dating stage. Holmes claims liberalism is performing well enough in its function of supporting a strong government when necessary, including attainment of social reforms, but otherwise restraining government through a civil society fortified by private property ownership.

12 Adam Michnik, "Gray is Beautiful, Thoughts on Democracy in Central Europe," *Dissent*, Spring 1997, 14–19. The article began as a talk at The New School of Social Research on Ira Katznelson's book, *Liberalism's Crooked Circle*, written as a letter to Michnik. In a brief response, Katznelson regrets Michnik has granted totalitarianism with a posthumous victory over the socialist legacy, but he leaves the door open.

13 In case there is any doubt about Michnik's steadfast turn away from socialism, see Michnik and Habermas, "More Humility, Fewer Illusions," 28:

Habermas: What are the prospects for the new [Kwasniewski] govern-ment?

Michnik: They will carry out policies that are more like Balcerowicz than

Balcerowicz himself. This is something I support, and not just in the hope that the pendulum will swing back to the right in the next election, but because it is the right policy.

9 China in Transition

When Deng Xiaoping died in February 1997, eight years after the fall of the Berlin Wall, the world turned its attention to a new center in the contest between socialism and capitalism. The voluntary march to capitalism in Russia, and in the key satellite countries of Hungary, Poland, and the Czech Republic, had irretrievably run its course. Only the tragic after-effects of the shock treatment remained. Economic corruption on a grand scale replaced Party corruption. A large poverty class, mainly the elderly and the unprepared, hung over the scene, victims of inflation and displacement, like similar casualties of revolutions and depressions destined to be forgotten by new generations. Ethnic and political factionalism, unleashed by democracy, flared up. Mourners for lost values, some principled, some trouble-makers, made their appearance. A cynical observer might declare these legacies of instant-democratic capitalism the least of the century's horrors, and remediable as well, given time and good fortune.

The Soviet collapse released the Western world from the fear of nuclear war, let alone threats to bury capitalism. The China experiment with markets, led by Deng from 1978 onward, with its variants such as "socialism with Chinese characteristics," and exotic strategies, such as "whether the cat is black or white makes no difference, so long as it catches mice," appeared more fascinating than threatening. In fact, a good deal of interest in poverty-stricken China had been dissipated with relief when Mao Zedong and the Russians clashed over ideology and border disputes in 1960 rather than mount a united front against the West. Nixon's mission to China in 1972 was frequently viewed as much opera as diplomacy.

134

Mao and Deng

Mao and Deng were larger-than-life figures, dominating China for twenty-nine and eighteen years respectively, far longer than the dozen years of Gorbachev and Yeltsin to date. Reasonable questions of transition strategy arise. Why didn't Russia follow Deng's gradualism? How far will China travel on the road to Western-style capitalism? Beyond such speculations, what happens in China, with one-fifth of the world's population, and a gross domestic product racing along at about 10% increase per year for a decade, will inevitably affect the future of democracy and capitalism in the Western world. A brief commentary on China's history in the time of Mao and Deng will set the scene.

Mao's improbable career includes a first phase as heroic soldier-statesman, the founding father of Communist China. This was followed by a second phase of absurd and terrible social experiments. He lived to age 83, a relentless egalitarian and cult-figure, far too long for his country's good. Deng died at 92, after four years of seclusion, but the "paramount leader" had placed China firmly on the road to economic reform, benefitting a very large segment of the population, at least 300 million. His flaw, by Western standards, was fear of democracy rather than capitalism.

* * *

Mao, born in 1893, came from a relatively prosperous peasant farming family. Intellectually ambitious, he left his roots to complete secondary school. At age eighteen, he spent six months as a volunteer with the local troops of Sun Yat-sen's revolutionary army, modestly participating in the 1911 bloodless overthrow of the hapless, archaic Manchu dynasty, led by the socialist, not Communist, first president of the Chinese Republic. This was the opening chapter in China's fifty years of war-torn trauma, involving two Japanese invasions (1915 and 1931), and protracted civil war between Communist armies and Kuomintang nationalists, led by Chiang Kai-shek, successor to Sun Yat-sen when the latter died in 1925. Mao emerged as the central character when the end of World War II removed the Japanese from China, leaving the ideological armies to fight for supremacy.

135

Ironically, not only the Allied victory played into Mao's hands, but American arms, liberally supplied to Chiang's nationalists, became a major arsenal for the Communists. Historians now claim that Chiang's troops, ill-fed and lacking motivation, continually surrendered their arms and ordnance for the benefit of Communist troops, in turn supported by millions of peasants, infused with the patriotism and promises of the People's Army. Chiang's conviction that the Communists represented a greater menace to China than the occupying Japanese insured his inglorious flight to Taipei in 1949. The Japanese, he claimed, attacked the body of China, but the Communists the heart. General Stilwell, assigned to coordinate Chinese troops against the Japanese as the war ended, reported this disastrous mind-set to Washington, unsuccessfully. In fairness, Chiang's delaying tactic of appeasement may have worked against Japan, regardless of second-guessing. How long could an invading army, at war with the US, hold down a continent with a population of about 500 million? At any rate, Chiang was a hero to the West, confronted with the handsome portraits of Chiang and his wife on separate covers of *Time*, then America's most influential periodical, and Madame Chiang's eloquent appeal before Congress. The Chiangs did not comprehend the strength of Mao's support from the awakened masses, directed against the elite class they symbolized.

* * *

The two antagonists for the control of China had worked together sporadically over the years before the final showdown in 1949, forming a united front against the repressive military regime that had displaced Sun Yat-sen in 1912, as well as the common enemy Japan. In this turbulent period of shifting alliances, Mao was not only a founder of the Chinese Communist Party but in 1925 the editor of the leading Kuomintang journal and a director of the Kuomintang Peasants Training Institute, an anomaly for Chiang, whose preferred power base was in the urban and landlord propertied class, not workers and peasants. In 1926, Chiang, wanting no rivals and solidifying his anti-Communism, reversed Sun Yat-sen's conciliatory policy and set out to annihilate Mao's 200,000 Red Army, now gathered in Jiangxi province with Mao as chairman of his own Chinese Soviet Republic. Eventually Mao was forced to abandon the fight, fleeing with 90,000 troops in 1934 to Yenan province, a 6,000-mile march to the cold northwest. The 5,000 survivors of the legendary exodus, including Deng, became mythologized as the Old Guard of the Chinese Communist saga. Even then, one more front against the Japanese was formally negotiated in 1937, when the Japanese began an attempt to subjugate all of China.[1] The uneasy alliance, which frustrated not only General Stilwell but later General Marshall, provided a training and recruiting period for Mao to establish the hardened army and peasant support that would eventually drive Chiang and a contingent of followers off the mainland to Taipei. By this time, the US had ceased supporting the Kuomintang, and Stalin, who had strongly pressured Mao to concentrate on the Japanese rather than Chiang, prepared to formally recognize his truculent counterpart.

The Great Leap Forward

Deng's twenty-two year apprenticeship in Mao's orbit involved surviving two career purges at the hands of the theory-obsessed "great helmsman." These shattering experiences helped make Deng a pragmatist and gradualist for the radical economic reforms he would bring to China.

There were other influences that separated the men, alike in their indomitable will and toughness. Deng, born in 1904, eleven years Mao's junior, was the son of a well-to-do rural landowner, with ancestry tracing to the Confucian-trained, mandarin officials who once looked down on Western barbarians seeking to trade with the imperial dynasties. At sixteen, he went to school in Shanghai and won a government scholarship for work-study in France. In 1920 France was mired in depression. The resourceful, small-statured foreign student earned his working-class credentials in a variety of jobs over a five-year period, from factory-worker to train conductor. In France he joined Zhou Enlai's Communist Youth League, convinced China needed radical change to rise again. He went on to Moscow for Marxist-Leninist indoctrination in 1926, the year Chiang turned his

137

Kuomintang forces against Mao's Communists. Returning to China, Deng met up with Mao and became his loyal follower. In the twists and turns of the Chinese party's relationship with their Russian overseers, both Mao and Deng were effectively banished in 1931 from leadership in a dispute over tactics, having advocated guerilla rather than conventional warfare against the Kuomintang. By 1934 they were leading the remnants of the Red Army in the Long March to the caves of Yenan.

* * *

The Great Leap Forward, (1958–1961), is of special interest to transition studies because it relates to a débacle of economic reform, resulting from Mao's self-perception as philosopher-king. In this role, he deemed himself capable of revising standard Marxist-Leninist theory, sparked by his antagonism to Russia's universal ideological claims in the first place. Mao had an intellectual as well as brutal side, typified by his favorite photos as Asian-Erasmus, seated at a plain desk, vertical stylus in hand, dressed in a Mao-style tunic, shorn of medals. In his youth he had spent a year at the University of Beijing, China's leading intellectual center, during the May Fourth Movement of 1919, calling for a turn away from Western liberalism, as China's destination, to dreams of "the world is ours" by way of Communist theory. He then returned to his home province for a year as grammar school-principal, but soon joined the Chinese Party, founded in 1921. Over the years, Mao edited a Kuomintang journal, as did Deng years later, and wrote books ranging from dialectical theory to military strategy. He achieved his author's peak through ceaseless editions of his Little Red Book, *Thoughts of Mao*, imposing his clichés and homilies on an entire nation, standard issue for every soldier, school-child, and household. A man of such colossal ego and mission was a natural candidate for the monumental and cruel aberrations of the Great Leap Forward and later the Cultural Revolution of 1967–1977. The pragmatic, cosmopolitan Deng, horrified by Stalin's immersion in self-cultism, disagreed but discreetly made sure first to survive, some-what like Gorbachev in Russia decades later.

For those interested in the subtleties of Marxist interpretation, Eric

Hobsbawm, the noted English historian, has a sharp eye for Mao's deviation:

...his ideal society [became] united by a total consensus...a kind of collective mysticism, the opposite of classical Marxism, which envisaged the complete liberation and self-fulfillment of the individual. Lenin never lost sight of the limitations of political action...Without [Mao's] belief that men could move mountains and storm heaven if they wanted to, the lunacies of the Great Leap Forward are inconceivable.[2]

One can add that Marxist-Leninism, while paying lip-service to the eminence of the proletariat, prescribed leadership from above, namely the vanguard of the Party elite, for marching orders. There is little to choose from between the rival camps. Mao's belief that he could harness the general will of China is a reprise of Rousseau's doctrine that inspired the terrors of the French Revolution. Both versions remind us that neither democracy nor capitalism can harbor the illusions of totalitarianism or utopianism without risk of destruction.

* * *

The details of the Great Leap Forward need re-telling, if only because the holocausts of modernity, from Atlantic slavery onward, must not be forgotten. The first phase was promulgated in 1958 for China's 90% agricultural sector, source of support for Mao's never-resting Red Army during the civil war. This vast population had legitimized Mao's Party-rule by virtue of its passivity whenever a period of order and peace became available, whether by mandate of emperors, warlords, or Party cadres. The trouble was Mao ordered overnight mass-collectivization, Russian-style, of the archaic peasant farms, landlords disregarded, without adequate preparation, time-tables, or investment in the necessary advanced machinery. Worse than that tactic, which could have been quickly amended or abandoned, cataclysmic droughts and floods appeared as if on schedule, bringing ruin and famine to most of the agricultural sector, with little left after the claims of the urban sector. Like all such disasters, for example, Stalin's ruthless liquidation of an entire farmer-owner class, now estimated at over twenty million, the number of victims slowly enter the history books. In China's case, official government statistics now indicate a two-year decline in population during the Great Leap in the range of forty million.[3] No one's hands were clean in the great famine. Zhou Enlai, the moderate, civilized top aide to Mao, who captivated the West on China's behalf, and was an apparent successor to Mao before his own death shortly before Mao's, marked time. Deng, further down the ladder, already known for favoring private plots of land and market initiatives for China's battered economy, avoided confrontation.

* * *

The second phase of the Great Leap Forward, also launched in 1958, was an effort to create thousands of miniature steel-mills in every village and township in China, galvanized by Mao's will and the untapped enthusiasm of the masses. Reflecting his mounting distrust of intellectuals and technocrats as well, or perhaps just his own dementia, Mao decided he could cause China to leap ahead to achieve the steel-making capacity of advanced, militarized economies. Even his estrangement from Russian collaboration at the time worked against him, as surely they were experts in such production. The bottom line, after a brief spurt, was a massive wreckage of existing metal structures and equipment to meet the quotas of the backyard forges, netting a useless output of inferior ingots. No regime ever achieves complete autonomy, and undoubtedly the steel-mills were sabotaged from the start.[4]

* * *

The Cultural Revolution (1967–1977)

The significance of these inane exercises in autocratic economic planning was not just the human tragedy, but Mao's resulting decision to punish the laggards in his own establishment, who he felt had betrayed him. His revenge was to transform and empower a whole new generation to replace the discredited authority of the old. The empowerment of children against their revolutionary elders is unique

140

in revolutionary history, but then Mao was an original force in the gallery of historic leaders.[5] This children's crusade was not a minor phenomenon, evoking images of teachers, elders, and intellectuals publicly humiliated in dunce-caps, reminiscent of Goya's etchings. For a searing indictment, consider the effect on higher education alone. It came to a virtual stop in the frenzy of anti-intellectualism. Whether enlisted in the Red Guards or not, children did not go to college for years. Mao, the self-appointed intellectual, was not the education chairman. In 1970, a high-year of the Cultural Revolution, total college enrollment is recorded at less than 100,000 in a population that had already rebounded to about 800 million.[6] When one speculates about whether or not Russia or China can survive the admittedly predatory and valueless aspects of the capitalism accompanying contemporary transition, it appears that these countries, veterans of worse catastrophes, can well survive capitalism, hostage as it is to new expectations.

The Cultural Revolution was Deng's Waterloo. In the midst of the daily accusations, he was branded a capitalist-sympathizer in 1966, forced to make the usual confession, and banished from the inner circles of the Party. His eldest son, a student at Beijing University, was beaten by Red Guards and tried to commit suicide by leaping from a window, becoming a paraplegic. Deng was spared by Mao, and confined to work in a tractor-repair facility in an infantry school in Jiangxi province, his departure point for the Long March with Mao thirty-two years earlier. In the crazy-patch atmosphere of Mao's dominion, after seven years in the wilderness, he was recalled by Mao to help shape up the military as vice-chairman of the Military Commission, and a vice-premier as well. Rehabilitated, he was sent to New York in 1974 to address the UN General Assembly, an opportunity to measure the world's market-system once again. Deng had one more obstacle course to run before he was home free. The unpredictable, aging Mao, always suspicious and jealous, turned on Deng once again, influenced by his wife and her Gang of Four. Deemed an enemy of the people, he was placed in political exile in April 1976, awaiting the next blow. Mao's death six months later gave him the unexpected chance to become China's instrument of miraculous economic reform. Deng seized control from Hua Guofeng, the interim Party chairman and president, and sent the unpopular Gang of Four to jail.

* * *

China as a Special Case in Transition

After escaping twice by the skin of his teeth in turbulent times, it is understandable that once in power, Deng desired stability and order above all, not to be found in an overnight conversion to complete freedom of press and assembly, or to civil rights and a multiple-party system. His apparent mission was to make China great and prosperous through market-reform without the distractions of Western-style political reform. This does not gather liberal support, especially in the light of his harsh suppression of popular dissent in the protest rallies for more democracy and less corruption in the Tiananmen Square rallies of 1989.

The preceding conditions in the various transition countries, and the personal experiences of their leaders, must be taken into account in any analysis of transition. They help us understand Deng on the one hand, and the predilection of Western leaders such as Yeltsin, Havel, Klaus, and Kwasnieski for the relative freedom of the market-system against the tyranny and inefficiency of the socialist command economy. They preferred democracy in partnership with capitalism.

In a larger sphere, considerations of national traditions and struggles remind us that capitalism itself rests on a spectrum of differences in background. They range from the American experience of a classless society of westward-bound entrepreneurs, the English concern for economic liberty against the encroaching state, the French success with the *dirigisme* of a state and business partnership, the Polish inheritance of a Catholic rather than Protestant ethic, and the Japanese ambition for economic supremacy to replace dreams of empire, again with state support. The list, of course, is incomplete, and the proposition is undoubtedly riddled with exceptions, but the differences are there.

What is a matter of modern consensus is that both capitalism and democracy are destructive agents, wherever they occur, for any old order or tradition. Alone or together, they constantly feed the winds of change, especially in the new world of advanced technology, travel, foreign students, and communications.[7] A good transition example would be Gorbachev's *glasnost* policy of democratic openness, resulting in the loss of Soviet satellites as well as his own position in the socialist order. China, unconcerned with building an empire in the name of Communism, can, like Singapore, South Korea and Taiwan, prosper indefinitely with an autocratic political system protecting its affair with capitalism. In the long-run, the pressure for more profits and technology, and for more personal freedom, will subvert this arrangement, but a long-run in the twenty-first century would be a good-run in itself. In China's case, with so much economic improvement awaiting delivery to its 1.3 billion population, economic progress and foreign trade will take priority over democracy.

Another consideration: Mao's one-party regime, for all its hare-brained experiments, was legitimated because it ended an obsolete, tyrannical, imperial system, bringing China into the modern world of men without pigtails, symbol of abject obedience, and of foot-bound women freed from their inferior position. It has not been shamefully totalitarian in the Western sense, to the extent its autocracy cannot be allayed by national pride, material improvement, increasing personal choices, and some token democracy in the villages. Whether it is home to capitalism or socialism with Chinese characteristics, it is a different variety of transition country, compared with Russia, Poland, Hungary or the Czech Republic. It is not a present candidate for Western-style democratic capitalism.

Deng's Achievement

Listed consistently by Freedom House as "not free," Deng's China nevertheless achieved spectacular economic reform and growth. The figures are familiar in the media, responding to the dictum that it's the economy that counts, at home or abroad, and magnified by the stock-taking after Deng's death, which closed an era in China. Since

143

widespread prosperity was the goal, some consumer items, from China's State Statistical Bureau, come first.

Per capita food consumption (in kilograms)

	1978	1995
Grain	196.0	97.0
Pork	7.7	17.2
Fresh Eggs	2.0	9.7

The first phase of reform was to end the communal agricultural system and allow immediate long-term and transferable lease of land. By 1990, China had its richest harvest ever, and the national diet shifted to less grain and new substitutes. Deng also introduced authoritarian population control, but China still increases at 30,000 per day.

Consumer durables (millions)

	1978	1996
Telephones	5.0	19.5
Radios	45.0	208.6
TVs	1.0	232.7

Automobiles in China

1978	1996
Practically none	2.5 million

We can also measure China by some of the standard transition categories used for Russia and the three former satellite countries.

Gross domestic product ($ billions)

1980	1994	1996	Average rate of increase per year
201	522	820	9% to 10%

China now ranks number seven in total GDP, above Canada and Brazil, but economic discussion centers on where it will be if it continues its present trajectory for another decade. Hong Kong will add another $130 billion to China's GDP, and brings with it a highly effective school for capitalism in the mainland.

* * *

Average annual increase in inflation (per cent)
1978–1995: 8.4
World Bank: From Plan to Market, 1996, Table 1.1

How did China manage to escape the horrible inflation that ruined a large segment of the most vulnerable, the old and the marginal workers, in the European transition countries? Agricultural prices were quickly freed at the beginning of Deng's reforms, and by 1992 there were no food price-controls in effect. The agricultural sector represented over one-third of GDP at the start, and 71% of employment, so it was a critical area.

Apparently good weather conditions, combined with financial incentives, resulted in tremendous production increases, satisfying the demand side without undue price pressure. There is also the discipline and fear an authoritarian government carries with it for exploiters, as the democratic countries well know from experience with temporary war-production endeavors. The World Bank, the leading foreign institutional authority on China's economy, considering China has been its number one customer for years, averaging $3 billion in loans annually, mostly for large infrastructure projects, contributes the following about inflation:

In effect, China followed a dual-track price reform system. As the state itself gradually reduced its own controlled-price purchasing and supplying, the non-state economy, including the newly-released agricultural sector, increased its purchasing and supplying of goods and service at market prices. The final convergence of the tracks ended with market-prices as the norm. This project was costly to implement and involved a vast number of bureaucrats to administer the system, particularly in relation to food prices, and was accompanied by severe penalties for corruption and non-compliance.[8]

Apparently Deng's *ad hoc*, experimental approach, relying on responses and adjustments from the ground up, with little dense theory from the top, of the type spelled out by economists and foreign-aid lenders in the European countries, worked very well. Deng acknowledged, in fact insisted, that he was no economist, but like FDR, he had a feel for what would work, or was worth the try. The gulf between gradual controlled inflation in China, and the ravages of hyperinflation in the European countries, is one for the history books. In this instance, the socialist system won the encounter. The experience flies in the face of the therapy-economists and their absolute conviction about transition strategies. In fairness, China's pragmatic economic reforms succeeded primarily because of the poverty-base from which they started, and the stable framework of a continuing political and economic system. The God of Wealth was on their side.

* * *

Town and Village Enterprises

Another unique transition strategy for China was the establishment of town and village enterprises (TVE's). This program accounts for a major shift in China's employment force, and a new quasi-private enterprise sector, supplementing the long-run, gradualist privatization of state enterprises. The latter takes place as it suits the state, cautious about adding to the millions of unemployed who have descended on the cities, seeking jobs and advancement.

The percentage of state employment in China remains at about 18% of the work force, while GDP has tripled, and the population expands. In Russia, state employment is less than 40% as a result of privatization, but GDP has plunged precipitously from the 1989 starting base, and population has decreased by 3.5 million. The following chart speaks volumes about China under Deng.

Where people work: percentage of total work force

	1978	1994
Agricultural	71	57
Industry	15	18
Services	14	25
	100	100

World Bank: From Plan to Market, 1996, Table 1

As the agricultural sector became more efficient, employment shifted to industry and services. How did China accomplish such mobility? Keep in mind Russia's 400,000 immobilized coal miners located in remote, inhospitable areas, unable or unwilling to move to new areas. China promoted new TVE's to engage this surplus work force in private or township profit-oriented, small-production units in nearby areas. The new rural industries generated 100 million jobs between 1978 and 1994, a pragmatic approach to the basic challenge of transition, providing employment, whether public or private. As the chart shows, the new prosperity also created a doubling of the work force in the services area, rural and urban.[9]

Meanwhile, further luck for China: The hand-to-mouth pre-conditions in the agricultural sector, and in urban life in general, did not generate money similar to the overhang of savings in Russia, which aggravated the inflation following the price liberalization finally bringing goods to market. As China's incomes improved, household savings and bank deposits grew rapidly. The new savers were satisfied with the low, non-inflationary interest rates available from the state banks, providing internal investment funds from the banks for modernizing industry. Additionally, foreign investors, led by the diaspora of Chinese enterprisers worldwide, with Hong Kong a major conduit, poured an immense $140 billion into China for job-creating ventures in the Deng period. It amounted to $40 billion in 1996 alone, beyond comparison with the funds received by Russia and the three former satellite countries, including foreign aid.[10]

An additional measure of transition-success lies in the increase in exports, which expand GDP through world markets, provide currency for buying technology, and reduce dependence on the need for import substitutions. China's exports, almost one-third in clothing and foot-wear, as store labels show, are now in the $130 billion area, compared with $120 billion in imports. The US, China's third-largest customer, is a major loser from such "unfavorable" trade balances, much reported in the press, and feared by those who claim a loss in US jobs. As a result of its export prowess, supported by low labor costs, China has accumulated a formidable $100 billion in international reserves to cover its exporting activity. The innovative TVE's account for over 30% of exports, testifying again to China's success on its own terms, despite reservations expressed by transition-authorities such as Jeffrey Sachs.[11]

Leaving China

China's economy is still in transition. It has one of the lowest GDP's per person in the world, and there is constant disparagement of its authoritarianism. The country is regarded as peaceful, even with a three-million army, and most speculation will center on its economy. What kind of market-socialism, the hybrid that eluded Gorbachev's best efforts, will exist ten years from now? Deng's technocrat-loyalist successor, Jiang Zemin, quickly announced there would be no change. The effect of Deng's personal history and innovative capacity was formidable. In 1992, age eighty-seven, with the economy slipping and inflation over 15%, partly arising from the conflict and uncertainty over the Tiananmen troubles, Deng surfaced to make a southern tour. He visited Guangdong province, an area the size of France, with a similar 60 million population, scene of his first major reforms, and showcase of China's economic miracle, both agricultural and industrial.[12] The effect was similar to FDR's fireside chats, not rational economics, but inspirational. There was immediate response from the region's liberated, decentralized entrepreneurs and bureaucrats, soon reflected in national statistics and on the Stock Exchange.

In Shanghai, a city of 16 million, site of another market-oriented, free-trade "economic zone," Deng's 1992 visit accelerated a fabulous boom in skyscrapers, subways, a giant airport, a massive stadium, even a $70 million art museum, netting a catch of world-class foreign manufacturers. Strangely repeating the disastrous race for highest cathedral in medieval France, a Japanese group is half-way up on a 95-story building, outcompeting the present Malaysian champion. If this isn't competitive capitalism, what is it? The 150-million farmers have long-term transferable leases, recently doubled to thirty years, in effect as good as private property and easier to acquire, as no-down payment auto-leasers will acknowledge. The China Stock Exchanges in Shanghai and Shenzhen, not yet booming because of gradualist restrictions, claim 21 million shareholders. Allowing for questionable statistics, this is not evidence of a nation of capitalists, any more than Russia's claim of shareholders is in that respect. But state-approved Stock Exchanges of even 10 million shareholders would not be listing shares in communes or cooperatives. They would list potentially profit-earning and possibly dividend-paying domestic corporations, further proof that China's market-socialism is in many respects a *de facto* capitalist economic system.

* * *

The Differences

What, then, are the essential differences between the European and China models, other than the gradualism allowed by China's pre-existing conditions? The first is the repression of democracy. Democracy, the Western countries claim, with its anti-state, property-owning, independent civil society, not only restrains the state, but enhances capitalism's need for an open, innovative society, in order not to regress Soviet-style. One of the unique aspects of China's case is that its adept and ingenious success with market-socialism mitigates that need. Presumably China has achieved heroic economic success without even pretenses of sufficient democracy, for those of us who place democracy first. How long Jiang Zemin and his closest advisors, who earned their credentials in administering Shanghai, will be able to travel on this path is a major question. Not only students and dissidents comprise the potential opposition. How much capitalist heresy will the hard-liner opposition allow? With only Mao and Deng as official icons, the flame of Communism burns brighter in the periphery, as is often the case, than the Marxist center. There must be millions of hard-liners still devoted to the anti-capitalist sentiments of these icons, however breached by Deng. Nor can the three-million army be considered an outpost for radical reform. The Chinese Constitution of 1982 clearly forbids the existence of private property. We can watch for its amendment or continued violation by the new administration.

There is at the same time a counter-current in favor of democracy,

149

aside from the uncertain claim that given time, authoritarian countries, once they achieve relative order and prosperity, largely through world trade, inevitably become democracies. China wants favorable economic treatment and great-nation recognition from the leading democracies, who in turn demand more democracy, in order to achieve the material goals necessary to satisfy the rising expectations of its awakened masses. Additionally, time is running out for the old order. The one-party choice on the ballot, regardless of democratic options in force at 80% of China's villages, is an anachronism. Party-rule, discredited in the Soviet débacle, does not wash well with the rapidly-growing, well-educated younger generations, the influential overseas Chinese, and the six-million voter-indoctrinated Hong Kong population.[13]

* * *

A second essential difference lies in privatization, the defining strategy for making the transition to capitalism, as described in chapter 5. Without comprehensive privatization, particularly of the larger firms, such as Russia's 18,000 firms employing 100 or more, there is no effective transition. The other factors of price liberalization, open-ing the door to foreign trade, allowing currency convertibility, elimi-nating state subsidies, imposition of budget restraints, and improved tax collection, have all been on China's agenda. In China's case, however, state employees started at 18% of the total work force on Deng's takeover, and continue at the same percentage in 1997. For transition purists, China's population increase in that period means 35 million more people on state-owned enterprise (SOE) payrolls, a highly negative position for market-theorists, even though the number of SOE's, mostly small units, has declined by half since 1985.[14] Jiang Zemin has listed privatization as a top priority, not to satisfy transition theory, but because state-ownership is the smoking gun of China's economy, first because of its extensive money-losing operations, and second, as the locus of profound corruption, the age-old partner of money and power, whatever the system. The money-losing state-owned enterprises are frequently reported as a fatal drain on the economy, and a threat to the entire state-banking system, which holds debt for the approximately 40% of the SOE's that are technically bankrupt, placing the banks in bankruptcy as well. Considerable privatization has already taken place for qualifying firms in the experimental economic zones. Guangdong province, for example, has sold 90% of its larger state enterprises to private owners, by direct offerings, not through voucher distributions favoring employees, as in Russia and the Central European examples. Many of these firms have been listed on the China and Hong Kong Stock Exchanges, and the accountability and drive for efficiency following the listings have been favorably noted. Still, privatization is the ultimate gamble, with as many as 20 million workers that may be downsized. Industrial workers, unlike the vast agricultural force, possess considerable social benefits. This will exacerbate the transition, but if China's dynamism and ingenuity run true to form, the transition will succeed, through gradualism, mergers of the fittest, and the creation of alternate benefits.

* * *

The pre-existing conditions and present differences that separate China from the former superpower Russia and the once-capitalist Hungary, Poland, and Czech Republic seem reasonably clear. Other than the control of hyperinflation, no major charges of failure can be made. There is, however, a common political denominator. The European transition countries struggled within the controlling restraints of an ongoing, obstructive political opposition, taking advantage of its democratic freedom. China's transition also depends on political action, in this case from the on-going authoritarian state. China's market-economy is not a command economy, but politics are in command in China. How else can one explain the boom in Shanghai, apparently without rational economic concern for overextended bank credit or the possibility of a near-term real-estate crash?[15] The aggressive hybrid-economy that is likely to prevail for several decades in China needs a new name, more complex than market-socialism.

Notes

1 Prior to the 1937 agreement, Chiang Kai-shek was kidnapped by his own officers, then released for the joint effort against Japan.

2 Eric Hobsbawm, *The Age of Extremes* (New York: Pantheon, 1994), 467.

3 China Statistics, 1989, Tables 3.1, 3.2, qu. by Hobsbawm, *The Age of Extremes*, 467.

4 In 1996, China reported it was first in world steel-production, displacing Japan. It also reported many of its state-owned steel enterprises were operating heavily in the red, excluding subsidies. (*Wall Street Journal*, 4 January, 1997, A12; *Economist*, 14 December, 1966, 61.)

5 Henry F. Kissinger writes he met personally with Mao, once with Nixon, then four times more in the next three years. "He exuded more concentrated will-power and determination than any other leader I have encountered, with the possible exception of General DeGaulle." (*Newsweek*, 3 March 1997.)

6 China Statistics, Tables 17.4, 17.8, 17.10, qu. by Hobsbawm, *The Age of Extremes*, 469.

7 More than 250,000 students have studied abroad, half in the US, since Deng opened the door in 1978. (China Statistics, *Los Angeles Times*, 7 April 1997, A14.)

8 World Bank, *From Plan to Market*, 1996, Box 2.2, 24.

9 World Bank, *From Plan to Market*, 1996, 21, 51.

10 World Bank, *From Plan to Market*, 1996, 4.

11 See Jeffrey D. Sachs and Michael Thye Woo, "Understanding China's Economic Reforms," Development Discussion Paper No. 576, Harvard Institute for International Development, (HIID), March 1997. Transition experts such as Anders Åslund, Richard Layard, Marshall Goldman, and Jeffrey Sachs, previously mentioned herein, are in agreement about why Russia and China are not comparable for transition experiences: China's pre-conditions, political continuity, dominant agricultural sector, limited social benefits, authoritarianism, small external debt, etc. For China itself, however, Sachs and Woo, in this recent report, suggest China will follow a different path than I have ventured. Briefly, they offer two options. One, China will continue its experimental, innovative, incremental path. Two,

a "convergence" school, which they endorse, sees partial reforms leading to "contradictions" in the economy (continued losses in the SOE's, or stagnation in agricultural productivity) sufficient to compel China to deepen its reforms and "normalize" its institutions to conform with its capitalist neighbors in East Asia. "Partial reform not only postpones confrontation with the most difficult problems (SOE losses and corruption), but also generates new tensions." In other words, China will have to move toward established market-theory and should stop temporizing. An elaborate World Bank study, *China 2020*, September 1997, supports this view.

12 See Ezra F. Vogel, *One Step Ahead in China, Guangdong under Reform* (Cambridge, Mass: Harvard University Press, 1989). In the great tradition of Harvard's world-class China studies, Vogel was immensely equipped to record Guangdong's reforms from 1978 to 1988. He had previously written *Canton under Communism*, and this would be its sequel. He enjoyed a network of China scholars and had a close relationship with members of the Provincial Economic Commission, who requested the study. He knew the language and customs and was frequently accompanied by his wife, Charlotte Ikels, equally at home in Guangdong, and a social historian and linguist on her own. No other foreigner has had such entrée and preparation to study a province in transition. His descriptions of the immense accomplishments in Guangdong and nearby provinces – cities the size of Boston built in a half-dozen years – emphasize the human resources of the Chinese as city-planners, architects, engineers, construction experts, and dedicated bureaucrats. Claiming a scholar's objectivity, he was given free rein. While he critically assesses certain "entrepreneurs, statesmen, scramblers, and niche-seekers," on the whole he finds "human socialism" adequate for the task at hand. Attracted to China's "noble civilization," he pays scant attention to democratic and environmental fault-lines, and is even less-concerned with free-market ideology, other than pragmatic free-market incentives. Professor Vogel, the Clinton administration's national intelligence officer for East Asia (1993–1995), has been an influential voice for moderation in policy towards China which he states is "America's most pressing international problem" in terms of potential impact. (See *Harvard Magazine*, March–April 1996, 38–39.) For an excellent journalist's report on China after Tiananmen, by an acknowledged authority, see Orville Schell, *Mandate of Heaven* (New York: Simon & Schuster, 1995).

13 An important change has apparently taken place in the composition and

attitude of the reigning Communist Party. It is still formidable, with 55 million members, up from 48 million in 1992. Yet a good percentage of its elite younger members resemble candidates for a Young President's Association, not the vanguard of the working-class. Deng's direction to recruit the best and the brightest has resulted in a major entry of educated career-seekers, motivated by Confucian principles of civic duty and moral integrity as much as by Marxism. Young intellectuals, once discredited in the Cultural Revolution, and further disillusioned by Tianenman Square, are now welcome and joining the Party, another chapter in the fluid China story. Ideology was further assaulted by Jiang Zemin's pronouncement at his inaugural Party Congress in September, 1997: "Deng Xiaoping Theory is the Marxism of present-day Thought." (See Rone Tempest, "In China, Red Party is a Shade of its Old Self," *Los Angeles Times,* 12 September 1997, 1.)

14 For market-theorists, see Jeffrey Sachs and Wing Thye Woo, "China's Transition Experience Reexamined," *Transition* (World Bank, March–April, 1996, 3; for number of remaining SOE's, *The Economist,* 14 December, 1996, 61.)

15 The urban and industrial sector explosion is augmented by macro-engineering projects for the country at large. For example, the Three Gorges Development, the world's largest hydroelectric project, estimated cost $29 billion, and new oil projects to carry oil from Kazakhstan, projected cost $6 billion, as outside energy needs are anticipated. As the leading customer for World Bank billions, roads, dams, and similar infrastructure are continually underway, creating employment but insuring more state-ownership at this level.

10 Russia Reconsidered

The disintegration of the Soviet empire and its Communist ruling-Party, after forty-three years of nuclear-age Cold War, is the overriding event, as well as the unexpected good fortune, of the century's end. In that perspective, it tends to modify excessive concern with the one-decade march to capitalism and democracy in the transition countries. Still, one tends to forget the near-catastrophe at the abyss, and to return to current speculations. When will Russia succeed in its reforms? What went wrong with its progress? How does its experience compare, not just with the liberated, revived satellites, but with China, the new economic transition-giant commanding the world's attention? Finally, is it time to reconsider the role of the state, after a prolonged period of free-market, anti-statist ascendancy, not only for transition countries, but for advanced capitalist countries?

* * *

This book started with Russia lurching towards capitalism and democracy, the beneficiary of $50 to $60 billion of Western aid, depending on one's scorecard, under the durable Yeltsin, after he assumed his herculean task in 1991. The former superpower has earned Freedom House credentials for democratic freedom, but few will deny it still lurches toward acceptable capitalism. I measure this in terms of restoring its depleted gross domestic product, the essential source of capitalist well-being, of attracting non-inflationary foreign investment, the hallmark of international confidence, of exporting high-quality industrial products, in order to become a leading

155

technological nation, of controlling corruption, and of providing tolerable employment for its once cradle-to-grave citizenry.

The lower 25% of this citizenry, displaced victims of hyperinflation and a vanishing state, constitute their own success story of fortitude and ingenuity. By scrounging along, doubling up with family, and conducting an immense underground, non-taxpaying economy, this poverty-index group has not defected at the polls to populists-nationalists in sufficient numbers to overthrow the new democracy. The unofficial economy, incidentally, is recognized as contributing 25% to the official GDP reported by government statisticians. By the same token, the powerful international-aid agencies now permit most of their own money, as well as foreign investment inflows, to qualify as bookkeeping adjustments for adherence to their budget-deficit goals, violations of which result in IMF suspension of its monthly $340 million payments. This is the bandaged Russia against whom the US created Star Wars. Ironically, in retrospect Reagan's threat is justified by many as pushing the Soviet economy to the point of self-destruction. Gorbachev himself was startled to learn his inherited defense item was 40% of his state budget, as noted in chapter 6. Russia's 50% reduction in the equipment and ordnance side of this item, at the expense of its ailing GDP, should be gratefully acknowledged. Its threadbare, bloated two-million man army is more dole than threat.

When Will Russian Reform Succeed?

Fortunately, the question is now a matter of time, not doubt. There are certain limitations even time cannot resolve. They include an orderly, peaceful succession when Yeltsin's term expires in 2000, or earlier. Otherwise, both capitalism and democracy may fail. Another temporal limitation: the $8 billion of committed foreign aid, still in the pipeline from IMF, World Bank, EBRD, the G-24 countries, even the modest annual amounts from the tight-fisted US, will terminate in another two years. Still, time is on Russia's side. The populace has now become too exhausted to contemplate more radical change, such as a return to the old system. They prefer freedom. The worst offence of shock

156

therapy, prolonged inflation, has finally settled down, eliminating a tinder-box of revolt.

In that setting, on the positive side there is the prospect of near-term economic normalcy for Russia, avoiding the temptress-word success. No fireworks, as in China, but a minimal expectation, based on a steady increase in GDP, widely anticipated, on providing private or even state employment at introductory low-wages for those wanting to work, incidentally aiding exports, and establishing a safety-net for others. Meanwhile, billions of Eurobonds, first sold by the government to meet expenses in 1996–1997, continue to be issued. Additionally, billions being bid by foreign investors, in a belated privatization of minority shares in Russia's major industries, a break with its previous xenophobic policy, are omens of success. These investors will demand efficiency for their money.

Finally, the remarkable renaissance of Moscow and other cities, under able administrators and their favored capitalists, large and small, is all to the good in this last stage of recovery, in a country still learning about democracy and the market-system.

* * *

The Negative Side

On the negative side, what kind of capitalism has Russia achieved after seven years of agonizing transition? Its quality-of-life index is marred by a 25% poverty-level, reduced life-expectancy, and increased crime, alcoholism and corruption, all largely remedial with better times. At the macro-economic level, however, the economy is plagued with paralysis, notably in the $8.8 billion owed by the government in mid-1997 to its own employees, pensioners, and private contractors, in effect making these groups unwilling financiers of the government's other expenses. Additional tens of billions are owed in arrears between large enterprises and their suppliers, running down the line to the weakest in the chain, as described in chapter 1. These unpaid billions are unique in economic history, let alone transition history. The explanation offered by some, such as the IMF,

157

that interenterprise arrearages represent the usual terms of payment in normal economies, does not help. In any event, the critical item of the $8.8 billion government arrearages must eventually be phased out by the state at all costs.

* * *

Income differentiation between the quick and the ready, on the one hand, and on the other, their generally elder opposites, mired in the coal-mines, for example, or in sub-standard employment, is well-known, and again will respond to better times. As troubling as the arrearages, however, is the dysfunction at the state level regarding fiscal affairs. The government has failed for years to meet modest, adjusted, deficit projections, including those for 1997. An obvious cause is the failure to collect taxes, an absolute necessity, once socialism is abandoned. One explanation lies in the outmoded and often confiscatory tax code, for years reported to be in process of complete overhaul. Another is the underground economy, too important for shock-treatment elimination. A more compelling reason is that the market-rules of commercial law and corporate openness have not caught on with the old *nomenklatura* of the autarkic, closed Soviet economy, a large number of whom were transformed into overnight capitalist managers, in the same firms of their prior lives. In reality, entrenched in power with captive employee votes, they are not subject to stockholder constraints, regardless of extensive privatization on the surface. Some sympathy must go to these managers, especially of the larger firms. They are reluctant to cut off their traditional company benefits, child-care and health-services, for example, until alternate services are provided. They cling to their status as important employers by paying token wages to employees who are often scrambling in the underground economy, picking up temporary unemployment benefits, or even stealing supplies for outside assembly and sale. The best of these managers will not create taxable profits in this situation.

All these infirmities are well-known to Yeltsin and the able, frequently-changed cabinet he has assembled. Men like Chubais and Nemtsov, or for that matter, Yeltsin and Chernomyrdin, understand the capitalist scenario, and would have made it to the top as executives in

158

any advanced capitalist country. By personal experience, they are on to the foot-dragging and tax-evasion of their pool of reluctant market-managers, and know what to do. The same can be said of the ever-present foreign-aid monitors, now liberated, by signals from headquarters, from the relentless free-market, anti-statist ideology guiding their initial years in Russia. The problem is how to motivate the inert economy without making it worse. Until a carefully-programmed, gradual sequence of forced-mergers, bankruptcies, management incentives and deadlines, and large-scale corporate downsizing, with appropriate fire-control benefits against the inevitable havoc, is taken, ultimate reform will be severely stalled, at great social cost. The reform will still succeed, in its present mode, because of the ruin nations can endure, as witnessed by recoveries from World War II, and the rise of a new phoenix like Vietnam.

The above regimen sounds easy enough, recalling the accomplishments of World War II emergency production-czars. This is a different war, where the enemy is no longer totalitarianism, and possibly not even socialism. It is economic gridlock in the surviving core of a socialist superpower, in a country where a good deal of the parliamentary opposition has an interest in the failure of the market-system.

Corruption

A word about corruption, since Russia appears to be a world-class leader in this underside of market-life. Larry Summers, US Deputy Treasury Secretary, a former World Bank official knowledgable about transition economies, estimates that 80% of Russian businesses make protection payments to criminal organizations. This might be tolerated as a remediable, transitory aspect of transition if it did not affect prospects for obtaining investment from abroad, attracted by Russia's low costs and great market potential. Such a stimulus to increasing GDP is reduced because of the additional investment risk in doing business in Russia. In language familiar wherever there is corruption, Summers assigns the blame to the top: "...government leadership must demonstrate that the rule of law will be applied evenly, and that even prominent and powerful people will be called to account."[1]

159

Russia's economic corruption is more serious than shakedowns. It not only involves tax-evasion, but accounts for capital flight, estimated at 40% of the annual $20 billion still leaving the cash-starved country for safe-havens abroad. The Russian Mafia reportedly has infiltrated the banking and financial systems and pockets millions of import duties through smuggling and bribery. They have acquired large interests in privatized industries, sold at auction to the highest, or probably in some cases, the lowest bidder. Their entrepreneurial talent might be useful as managers, but they are attracted to stripping-off assets for their own pockets, forgetting other shareholders, and the tax-collector as well. Finally, corruption leads to crime. An incredible number of businessmen, high and low, are murdered in Moscow annually, mostly in internecine warfare. At the very top, in 1995 alone, the Russian Business Roundtable lost nine of its thirty officials to assassination.[2]

This perfunctory treatment of a major problem reflects the belief that corruption is a stage of the market-system that eventually can be contained, wherever it occurs, by energetic state regulation, and is less serious than the fiscal gridlock described above. In China, Jiang Zemin's former powerful ally, the ex-Mayor of Beijing, has recently paid the price for corruption, and the *Wall Street Journal* is a constant chronicler of such news, at home and abroad.

The New Oligarchs

The new oligarchs are multi-millionaires – some say billionaires, at least on paper – who enjoy the celebrity status once reserved for commissars and cultural heroes. The Big Seven of this group reportedly control as much as one-third of GDP. More accurate figures must await the arrival of greater *glasnost*, or openness, in the economic area, when the institutions and rules of regulated capitalism will inevitably follow the frontier stage.

These robber barons, or monopolists, or captains of industry, depending on one's view, are not corrupt, until proven so. In fact, it is difficult to conceive of them submitting to, or conniving with, petty shakedown organizations. *Forbes Magazine* accused one of the most notable oligarchs, Boris Berezovsky, of Mafia-ties in 1996. He responded with threats of an appropriate suit, but *Forbes* held its ground. Berezovsky then returned to profit-seeking and in 1997 to a top spot in Yeltsin's cabinet, after the Big Seven contributed generously and openly to Yeltsin's reelection campaign.

As a group, these oligarchs are young, energetic, and highly-talented.[3] They put their money, and often their lives, on the line. They require bodyguards and send their sons to study abroad. Perhaps some envision themselves as founding families, like the Kennedys, whose next generations will turn to philanthropy, public office, and other warrants of respectability in the mobile society that has given them their chance. Berezovsky has recently announced he has placed his conflict-of-interest holdings in a public trust, sensing trouble ahead. Never reticent, he has referred to himself and his colleagues as the "the magnificent seven."[4] A common denominator: they have used their privately-owned, unregulated banks, as far as possible, to assemble and finance their empires.

Their objective apparently is to whittle their companies into shape, like merciless American corporate-doctors, and make their fortunes the new way, by market-appreciation of listed shares related to future earnings. In their special arena, fighting with each other over targets and territory, it is likely that only three of the seven will be forces a decade from now. They are only pale imitations of the great Japanese and South Korean combines, which include industry-building giants like Matsushita and Samsung. They differ immeasurably in terms of scale, innovation, integration, resources, and decades of government industrial-policy on their behalf. Many of the Russian Big Seven assets were acquired in a second or third round of bargain ownership, or at bailout prices and terms directly from a government desperate to unload certain dinosaurs and their subsidized overhead. On balance, however, they have made a remarkable current contribution, unleashing the invaluable "animal spirits of capitalism" J.M. Keynes recognized from such endeavors.

Eventually Yeltsin and his enlightened new team will read the riot act to the Big Seven, lightning rods for public hostility and political unrest. They will lose their positions of favoritism and cronyism, probably to their advantage. Unwisely, the Big Seven have crossed another boundary at odds with democracy. They have acquired widespread ownership in newspapers, TV and radio.[5] The agents of Russian political reform did not contemplate substituting one method of thought-control for another. In time there will be forced divestitures.

The China Model

Typically, Russia's transition has been compared with results in the key former Soviet satellites, such as Poland, Hungary, and the Czech Republic. In this exercise, standard categories of inflation, GDP, foreign investment, privatization, and the poverty-index are applied, beginning with the imposition of shock therapy in 1989–1991. At that starting point, the satellites had much in common with Russia, after forty-three years of command socialism, ruthlessly and often skillfully administered from Moscow. Apples were compared with apples.

If the China model was raised, it was to note the differences in pre-conditions, such as China's overwhelming agricultural population, its continuing authoritarian political system, its lack of external debt, and its disinterest in democracy, in order to avoid comparison. Meanwhile, the free-market formula, based essentially on belief that the market will provide equilibrium at an appropriate level, absent state inter-vention, prevailed. It was advocated by foreign-aid experts in the IMF and World Bank, and promoted conceptually by the highly-visible and articulate transition-authority Jeffrey Sachs, along with able disciples in each country. They were reasonably successful in the satellite coun-tries. They were not in Russia, considering the seven lean years in that country so far, and the major social costs.

Today, the China model is in the forefront of transition news. It is the all-time year-to-year GDP winner. It has transformed its agri-cultural sector immeasurably, shifted millions into new occupations and created a remarkable record in small and large industry growth, in exports, and in city-building. It is a country with similar time-zone problems as Russia, and with less literacy, technological experience, and natural resources. All this was achieved with controlled inflation.

For further comparison, China has been the recipient of substantial

162

annual funds from the World Bank, on a non-ideological basis, qualifying for such treatment on a humanitarian basis, so far, because of its low GDP per capita. Meanwhile Russia deservedly received $50 to $60 billion of transition-aid from the West, delivered with free-market strictures, and billions more in debt abrogation from foreign governments and banks.

All in all, it is tempting to ask the unasked. Why did not Russia emulate, in the past ten years, to a far greater extent, its Asian prototype? Why did it not, like Deng, take what it wanted from the model on the other side of the ideological road?

One answer must lie in the aversion to a model strongly committed to Communist Party-rule, an obstacle which the Russian reformers had to rid themselves of, economically as well as politically, to meet their new destiny. We have used a similar existential fact to explain why Havel and Michnik, recalling their own imprisonment, opted for the immediate free-market model as consistent with their yearning for democracy. Still there are cases where economic reformers expediently overlook past antagonisms. Ezra Vogel makes it clear that South Korea, for example, emulated above all the hated Japan's techniques and economy, because they worked so well.[6] On the other hand, Gorbachev's rejection of Deng's obvious decade of success in granting land and opportunity to his liberated agricultural sector was made on the basis of Gorbachev's loyalty to the socialist anathema against private property.

Granted Yeltsin and his advisors in turn had reasons to steer clear of China's Communist Party-statist model, in hindsight where could they have followed it advantageously? Unquestionably, gradualism in price liberalization would have been a better choice. We have detailed China's two-track, controlled sequence regarding prices in chapter 9. Russia's economy was unprepared, by tradition and structure, to gamble with such an exposure to ruinous hyperinflation. The accompanying failure of the state to impound or exchange for government notes the overhanging cash stashed away at all levels, high and low, exacerbated the offense, as noted in chapter 1. For once the elaborate time-servers and statisticians in the bloated bureaucracy were in place to guide through a two-track, gradual liberalization, and to harshly restrain profiteers. That Poland, Hungary, and Czechoslovakia put out

163

their anticipated inflationary fires in time does not prove the case for Russia. There are many types of market-systems and capitalist-systems in evolution throughout the world. There was no need to attempt to create a price-free capitalist order in time-frozen Russia in seven days, at the cost of seven dreadful years.

* * *

Similar second-guessing applies to Russia's experience with privatization, the defining strategy of transition, the shift from state-owned to privately-owned means of production. Obviously, small enterprises, up to twenty employees, could have been overnight gifts or insider sales to their operators, with free access to all new entrants in private enterprise, risking their own money, and paying taxes, at any level. The rest of the state-owned firms should have been divested in more deliberate stages with market rules and regulations, and management-standards, as in the China model. Privatization would have then reached the sensible present program of Yeltsin and his chagrined advisors in the first two or three years of transition, not six years later, when looters and unprepared *nomenklatura* still occupy a large part of the moribund economy. It is not a convincing argument that China's gradual privatization has only recently started. China's long-range program was officially cited in Yeltsin's early years, and 90% of larger state-owned industries had been privatized in the experimental economic-zone of Guangdong province, with its 60-million population, by 1988. In retrospect, the extraordinary self-congratulations of the top lieutenants in Chubais's privatization program were unwarranted, aside from the speed and daring of the operation. They claimed that otherwise the opportunity would be lost.[7] A quasi-official follow-up was made by the Russian National Survey, a well-financed team of American and Russian experts, who personally visited 679 firms privatized from 1992–1996, averaging 2,000 employees, throughout the country. Starting out to show the best front, the examiners cannot conceal their disillusionment after a four-year survey, mainly for the reasons advanced in this chapter. They cannot comprehend that two-thirds of the general managers said they would discourage selling a majority of shares to outside investors in return for a necessary infusion of new capital: "This mentality is suicidal. It makes no business sense."[8] The surveying-authors of the report come to a "...shocking conclusion... Three-quarters of these corporations need radical and far-reaching restructuring...at least a quarter should be bankrupt."[9] In summary, although the privatized managers had stock interests, they did not feel secure or understand their role. Supply and sales networks had been shattered by the breakup of the Union. Most of them lacked skills in marketing and financial management. Again, in hindsight, privatization in Russia was a difficult trade-off, but it could have been far better, with more reliance on the state and less on the market as self-correcting agent.

The Role of the State

The changing role of the state is critical at several levels. The global-economy is concerned with footloose, less-than-patriotic multi-nationals, with runaway monetary systems, prey for hunters like Soros, with epic trade conflicts, overpopulation, and environmental doom, all calling for uncharted state and supra-state intervention. At the national level, the absolute priority of jobs at home, and economic power as an instrument of foreign policy, are self-evident, requiring constant evaluation of state presence or absence.

In this setting, where the state appears likely to be summoned again for a new round of economic service, a judgment about the economy in the Cold-War years can readily be stipulated. There is no question, and much proof, that elimination of excessive state interference, including tax-reduction and a turn to privatization, reached a peak of popularity and accomplishments in the Reagan-Thatcher era. Less intervention resulted in more efficiency, more initiative, more pride in property, and more wealth for a broad segment of the population, regardless of the stimulus of record defense-spending. Whether planned or fortuitous, like other economic cycles whose time had come, there was a triumph of market-capitalism, brought into glaring focus by the débacle of socialism, that helped raise the market-system to a kind of theology.

The trend has apparently capped, as shown politically in the

165

elections of Clinton, Blair and other reconstructed left-of-centrists. Moreover, those nostalgic for a revival of overdue regulation, and more comprehensive welfarism, should note that the state never really abandoned its role in the first place. An ideological journal, *The Economist*, reviewing the role of the state in depth, acknowledges these counter-intuitive statistics, in the high-tide of free-market resurgence:[10]

The role of the state – G-7 countries
Government spending as % of gross domestic product

	1980	1996
Canada	38.8	44.7
France	46.1	54.5
Germany	37.9	49.0
Italy	41.9	52.9
Japan	32.0	36.2
UK	43.0	41.9
US	31.8	33.0

This is hardly a vanishing state. Treated separately, social services and welfare transfer-payments alone averaged 25% to 30% of budget. What of the reverse role of the state as tax-collector? An average one-earner couple, with two children, paid the following top marginal-rate of taxes on wages in this period, in the G-7 countries:

1978	1995
36.2	38.7

The sky did not fall down, in spite of the heavy-handed taxing and spending. This was largely due to the increase in GDP, regardless of such impediments. Granted such statistics tell only a partial story. A great deal of GDP success relates to shifts in the state's role within the components, for example, the beneficial results expected from work-fare rather than welfare, by tax reductions and education-benefits provided for the lower percentile of taxpayers in the unskilled workforce, and devolution of central functions to lower or privatized levels. Still, the state is very much with us.

Russia as a Transition Laboratory

The changing role of the state will greatly define the future of democratic capitalism. Russia's transition experience provides a valuable laboratory, with a beginning and end. There one can examine the ongoing, constructive conflict between free-market ideology and experimental pragmatism in relation to the economy.

How did Russia become a case-history largely governed by free-market ideology? The central role of the IMF and World Bank must be recognized. These non-governmental agencies, although controlled by the minority shares of the G-7 countries, dominating the 180 member-countries, entered a vacuum created when the Western world dawdled in indecision and broken promises about how to help the transition in the wake of the unexpected Soviet disintegration, about the time of the Persian Gulf War. Avoiding national legislatures, they boldly fulfilled a function never intended by their charters. With massive funds at their disposal, and employing the world's largest pool of highly-skilled technocrats, they doled out at least $50 billion on their own, if we include the former satellites and the newly-independent states surrounding Russia, in less than a decade, after a slow start. This unique operation differed radically from United States largesse under the Marshall Plan after World War II. Marshall Plan cash grants and commodity credits were made outright, not evidenced by deferred-payment loans, as with the aid-agencies. Nor were they influenced by ideology. The US had pragmatic motives, beyond its genuine humanitarianism, to contain the threat of Russia, and to provide a market for future exports. Completing the irony of the current transition-aid, many prominent observers assert such agencies, at least the World Bank, would not be established today. In the World Bank's case, aside from duplication of some IMF functions, they cite the unprecedented availability of foreign investment funds, and the possibility of contracting out to private firms the infrastructure projects the Bank provides to poorer countries.

Here is where ideology enters the picture. It stands to reason that these agencies, responding to the triumph of the market-system in democratic countries during the Cold War, could be expected to include such ideology as a quid-pro-quo for their money and

167

brainpower. A free-market transition-authority like Jeffrey Sachs might publicly scold the IMF for "betrayal," but only because of too little and too late, or flawed techniques, not for ideology.[11]

I have suggested in chapter 3 that if an international figure like Havel had been placed by G-7 leaders at an international cabinet level, above the IMF and World Bank bureaucracies, a more European cast of mind, less absolute about shock therapy and more open to gradualism and pragmatism, would have cushioned Russia's agony. The availability of the China model was on hand.

* * *

A noteworthy modification in the World Bank's ideology came from President Wolfensohn in 1997. The IMF, specializing in monetary stabilization and foreign trade imbalances, nevertheless became team-leader at the start of funding in 1991, emphasizing the state's role to withdraw from the economy wherever possible. President Wolfensohn assumed his post in 1995, facing an entrenched army of 10,000 employees engaged in a worldwide development program. The Bank's literature for years had advocated a free-market, anti-statist policy, although its most-favored client, China, hardly fit the billing.

In announcing a belated, unexpected $6 billion aid-program for Russia in early 1997, the Bank called on the state to use the money in a joint effort to alleviate the great social dislocation that had disfigured the reform. A June 1997 report, *The State in a Changing World*, carried the President's message:

> ...Many have felt the logical end of all these reforms was a minimalist state. Such a state could do no harm, but neither could it do much good...The Report shows how opportunities for reform can open, and widen, with the help of careful sequencing of reforms and mechanisms to compensate losers.[12]

The Bank's admirable self-examination, assuredly made in a wider context, does not prove or disprove claims about Russia's difficult transition. It does, however, remind us that the role of the state continues to be paramount in the ongoing development of democratic capitalism.

Instead of absolute theory, a more pragmatic approach, based on a country's needs, traditions, and stage of growth, is strongly advocated.

Notes

1 *Transition (World Bank)*, February 1997: "Larry Summers Prods Russia to Resume its Reform Agenda," 5–6; see also "The Global Stake in Russian Economic Reform," address to US-Russia Business Council, 1 April 1997.

2 Blasi, Kroumova, Kruse, *Kremlin Capitalism*, 119.

3 Strobe Talbott, US deputy secretary of state, a key supporter of Yeltsin's Russia, regards the 65% approval rating of the younger generation (under 35) as "the most significant and hopeful statistic about Russia today...The essence of US policy is give them time." *Wall Street Journal*, 25 September 1997, A22.

4 *Transition (World Bank)*, April 1997, 11.

5 Who are the overnight capitalists? Three of the Big Seven will suffice:

Boris Berezovsky, 51, former mathematician, now an auto-tycoon, with investments in oil and air travel, owns 16% of the largest national TV network, 50% of the weekly magazine *Ogonyok*. Survivor of car-bombing.

Vladimir Goussinsky, 44, former engineer and theatre director, founder of Most Bank in 1989, now one of the largest in Russia, considered a media czar, involved in 40 diversified businesses.

Vladimir Potanin, 36, former bureaucrat, founded Uneximbank, Russia's largest private bank, controls large oil and metals producers. In July 1997 merged his Bank MFK with his Renaissance Capital securities firm, to form Russia's largest financial group, with $2 billion in assets. In and out of Yeltsin's government.

To further complicate Russia's industrial web, the government in 1996 encouraged and authorized over 50 "financial and industrial groups" (FIG's), which appear to be informal holding companies of financial and like-industry members, seeking to produce Russian-style multinationals, while lobbying for government support.

6 Ezra Vogel, *The Four Little Dragons, The Spread of Industrialization in East Asia* (Cambridge: Harvard University Press, 1991), 47–50.

7 Boycko, Schleifer, Vishny, *Privatizing Russia*, 152–153.

8 Blasi, Kroumova, Kruse, *Kremlin Capitalism*, 179.

9 Blasi, Kroumova, Kruse, *Kremlin Capitalism*, 178.

10 *The Economist*, 21 September 1997, *The Future of the State*, 5–47.

11 Jeffrey Sachs, "Betrayal," *The New Republic*, 31 January, 1994, 14–18.

12 *World Bank Development Report 1997, The State in a Changing World*, Foreword by James D. Wolfensohn, President, 30 May 1997.

Index

171

173

174